For my grandchildren:

Ciara, Amy, Emer
and Conor

MAPS

TWISTS OF FATE

Stories Behind Irish Battles and Sieges

JOHN McCORMACK

MENTOR
BOOKS

First Published in 2005 by

MENTOR BOOKS
43 Furze Road,
Sandyford Industrial Estate,
Dublin 18,
Republic of Ireland.

Tel: + 353 1 295 2112 / 3   Fax: + 353 1 295 2114
e-mail: admin@mentorbooks.ie
www.mentorbooks.ie

ISBN 1-84210-244-3

A catalogue record for this book
is available from the British Library

Cover by: Anú Design

Edited by: Una Whelan

Design, layout and illustrations: Nicola Sedgwick

Printed in Ireland by ColourBooks Ltd.

1 3 5 7 9 10 8 6 4 2

CONTENTS

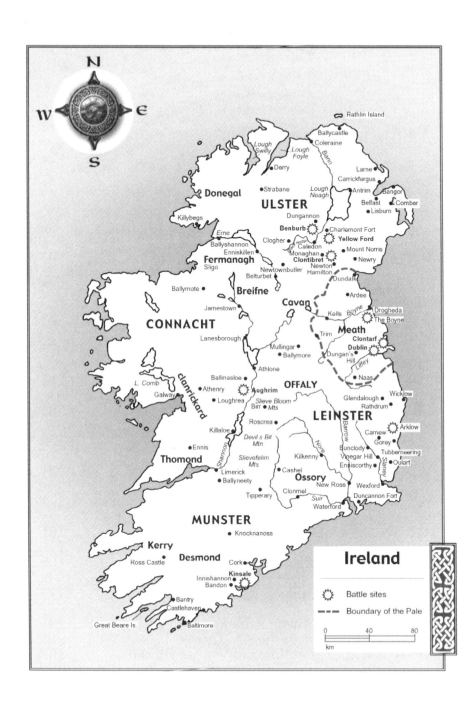

N
W E
S

Rathlin Island

Ballycastle
Lough Swilly
Lough Foyle
Coleraine

Derry
Larne
Carrickfergus

Donegal
Strabane
Lough Neagh
Antrim
Bangor

ULSTER
Belfast
Comber

Killybegs
Dungannon
Lisburn

Benburb
Charlemont Fort

Erne
Clogher
Caledon
Yellow Ford

Ballyshannon
Enniskillen
Monaghan
Mount Norris

Fermanagh
Clontibret
Newry

Sligo
Newtownbutler
Newton Hamilton

Belturbet
Dundalk

Ballymote
Breifne

Jamestown
Ardee

Cavan
Kells
Boyne
Drogheda
The Boyne

CONNACHT
Meath

Lanesborough
Trim
Clontarf

Mullingar
Dublin

Ballymore
Dungan's Hill

Athlone
Liffey

Ballinasloe
Naas

L. Corrib
clanrickard
Athenry
Aughrim
OFFALY

Galway
Loughrea
Slieve Bloom Mts
Glendalough
Wicklow

Birr
Rathdrum

Roscrea
LEINSTER

Killaloe
Devil's Bit Mtn
Carnew
Arklow

Ennis
Slievefelim Mts
Kilkenny
Bunclody
Gorey

Thomond
Vinegar Hill
Tubberneering

Limerick
Enniscorthy
Oulart

Ballyneety
Cashel
Ossory

Tipperary
Clonmel
New Ross
Wexford

Suir
Duncannon Fort

Waterford

MUNSTER
Knocknanoss

Kerry
Ross Castle
Desmond
Cork
Kinsale

Innishannon
Bandon

Bantry
Castlehaven

Great Beare Is.
Baltimore

Ireland

Battle sites

Boundary of the Pale

0   40   80
km

The BATTLE *of* CLONTARF

(April 1014)

The Battle of Clontarf happened so long ago that it is hard to distinguish fact from legend in the accounts of the battle.

Early Norse Raids

Several names have been used by historians for the Scandinavian adventurers who started their raids on Ireland in 795 AD. They are known variously as Norsemen, Danes, Ostmen (Old Norse for 'men of war') or *Lochlannaigh* (Gaelic for 'men from the land of lochs'). Sporadic hit-and-run attacks took place subsequently at the rate of about one a year until about 830 AD when much larger fleets sailed into the Liffey, Shannon, Erne and Boyne. These Norse forces stayed in Ireland for weeks or months before returning home. Later raids resulted in permanent settlements.

Brian Boru, High King of Ireland

Many battles were fought against these raiders and the most

The Vikings who raided Ireland came mostly from the coasts of Norway and Denmark. Early Irish writers called those who came from Norway *Fionnghaill* (White Foreigners), and those from Denmark *Dubhghaill* (Black Foreigners). In popular language in Ireland they were referred to as Danes, while in England they were called Norsemen, Vikings or Ostmen.

The first Viking raid in Ireland is said to be that on the monastery on Lambay Island in 795.

The Vikings established a *longphort* (ship harbour) at Annagassen in County Louth in 841 AD. They also established settlements at Drogheda, Waterford and Limerick during the following century.

Among the many monasteries raided by the Vikings in the eighth and ninth centuries were those at Scattery Island off the coast of Clare, Bangor in County Down and Clonmacnoise in County Offaly. They are also said to have plundered the famous passage graves in the Boyne Valley.

famous of these was the battle of Clontarf in 1014 AD. According to the annalists, Gormflaith, the sister of Maolmordha, King of Leinster, and mother of Sitric, the Danish King of Dublin, had mocked her brother for cowardice in agreeing to pay tribute to Brian Boru when the latter became High King of Ireland in 1002.

The Viking ship. Because of its shallow draught it was equally at home on the high seas and rivers and lakes.

Some time later Maolmordha was on a visit to Kincora, Brian's palace near Killaloe, when a bitter row developed between himself and Brian's eldest son, Murchadh. Maolmordha stormed out of Brian's court vowing vengeance for the insults he claimed to have received. Back home he roused the Leinstermen and Norsemen against the High King and, together with a few neighbouring chieftains and some Dublin Danes, began to attack King Malachy of Meath, who was one of Brian's adherents. Brian then laid siege to Dublin but was forced to withdraw as the weather was deteriorating and his food supplies were running short.

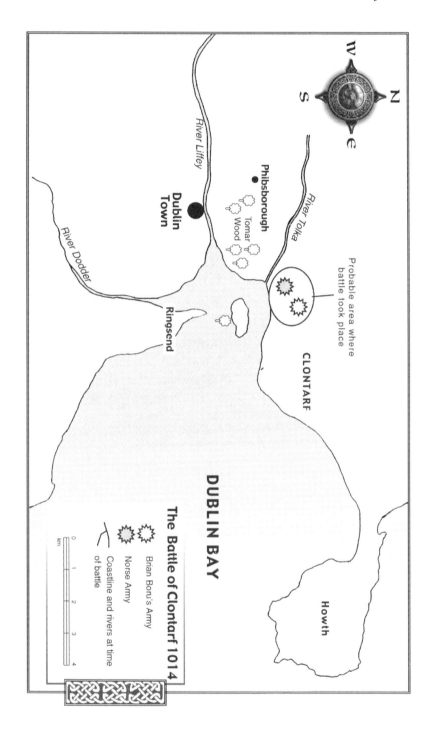

The Battle of Clontarf 1014

Brian Boru's Army

Norse Army

Coastline and rivers at time
of battle

km   0   1   2   3   4

DUBLIN BAY

Howth

CLONTARF

Probable area where
battle took place

River Tolka

Phibsborough

Tomar
Wood

River Liffey

Dublin
Town

Ringsend

River Dodder

Maolmordha and Sitric knew that Brian would again collect an army and renew the attack the following year, so they made preparations to be ready for him.

Gormflaith contacted Brodir, the leader of the Danes in the Isle of Man, Sigurd, the Norse ruler of the Orkneys, and other Norse leaders, asking them to come to Ireland to defeat the High King.

Brian, who was seventy-three years old (a great age for the time), was reluctant to continue the struggle but the longer Leinster remained independent the greater was the threat to his rule. Although the annalists would have us believe that Brian's call for assistance was willingly answered by all the other provinces, in fact his main support was from Munster and some rather conditional assistance from Malachy of Meath. Even so, Brian's forces were far superior in number to those of his enemies.

The numbers engaged on both sides in the Battle of Clontarf have been the subject of considerable debate. The annalists claimed that Brian's army numbered 20,000 men and that 14,000 of the enemy were slain in the battle. (The total numbers of both Saxon and Norman armies at the Battle of Hastings, half a century later, totalled no more 9,000 men, so Clontarf, a much smaller event, probably involved about 5,000 men altogether.) Nevertheless, the Battle of Clontarf was to be one of the fiercest fought in Ireland to that date.

Brodir Arrives

On Palm Sunday, April 18, 1014, a large Norse fleet, led by Sigurd, sailed up the Liffey in Dublin. Also in the party was Brodir, at the head of a force of brigands. It is difficult to establish how many were in the invading force but it is probable that they were numbered in hundreds rather than thousands.

According to the Norsemen, Gormflaith was 'the fairest of all women'. They also said, however, that 'she did all things ill over which she had power'.

Even though the Vikings were the first to mint coins in Dublin, it seems that generally they did not have much use for them. They did not carry purses and are supposed to have concealed coins in times of danger by sticking them to armpit hair with beeswax.

Not many Norse words entered the Irish language. Most of those that did are connected with sailing, fishing or trading: *pingin* – a penny, *scilling* – a shilling, *ancaire* – an anchor, *bád* – a boat, *beor* – beer, *fuinneog* – a window, and *margad* – a market are some examples.

Among items discovered in archaeological digs in Dublin in 1970 were finely woven hair nets dating from Viking times. It was also discovered that the diet of the inhabitants included beef, pork, grain, wild nuts, berries and figs.

Vegetables commonly used by the Vikings were onions, cabbages, parsnips, peas, beans and leeks.

Brian's first objective was to contain the enemy within the Dublin area. He was so confident of his numerical superiority that he sent a small part of his army to Wicklow, under the command of his son, Donnchadh. This was meant as a warning to the chieftains in south Leinster not to support Maolmordha.

Brian established his headquarters north of Dublin at what is Phibsborough today; at that time all of the town of Dublin lay south of the Liffey. The Norse army, meanwhile, occupied a sloping plain north and east of the River Tolka towards Clontarf. The Tolka flows eastwards towards the sea and near the present-day Ballybough was the little weir of Clontarf. It was around this weir that the battle was fought – in fact the battle was called the 'Battle of the Weir of Clontarf' in some chronicles.

When Brian arrived in Phibsborough he held a council of war and immediately afterwards Malachy withdrew his forces. It is not known why he did this but everything points to a quarrel between him and Murchadh, the son of Brian Boru. Brian next summoned Donnchadh to make haste to return from Wicklow with fresh troops. The departure of Malachy and the prospective arrival of Donnchadh prompted Sigurd and Brodir to start hostilities immediately.

The Battle Commences

The battle itself seems to have been a whole series of hand-to-hand encounters, with no tactical disposition of troops on either side. Brodir is said to have 'gone through the host of the foe and felled all the foremost that stood there' until he came up against a man named Wolf who 'struck him down three times'. Brodir then fled from the field to the nearby Tomar wood.

Legend has it that when Brian Boru became High King of Ireland the country became so peaceful that a beautiful young lady, richly dressed, and bearing a gold ring on her hand, travelled the country from north to south without being molested. Thomas Moore later wrote a song about the event – 'Rich and rare were the gems she wore.'

Strangely enough, in view of the description of the Viking army which fought the Normans, no body armour from Viking times has been discovered in Dublin archaeological digs but iron swords, spearheads, axeheads, and large numbers of decorated bronze pins and combs made from bone or the antlers of red deer, have been found.

The Norsemen favoured a short-handled, wide-bladed axe which could be held with both hands and which caused terrible damage in close encounters.

According to the annalists, Brian's army was so closely arranged together that a four-horse chariot could be driven on their heads from one side to the other.

With the passing of the years more foreigners intermarried with the native Irish. Both the Vikings and the native Irish practised bigamy. It was considered a status symbol to have more than one wife. When young Viking men were seeking a wife they grew their beards long and used make-up on their eyes.

From early morning until sunset the struggles continued with each side using swords, short-shafted, wide-bladed axes, and javelins, while many of the combatants had a rudimentary armour made of leather, reinforced with metal studs and rings.

Gradually the forces of Brian gained the upper hand and Sitric, seeing the way things were going, emerged from Dublin with his army to assist his fellow-countrymen. His men were overwhelmed too, and Sitric himself was lucky to escape with his life. Maolmordha did not manage to escape, however, but it is not known at what point in the battle he was slain.

One notable casualty on Brian's side was his son, Murchadh. Towards the end of the day he encountered a Norse leader called Amrud and engaged him in hand-to-hand combat. Murchadh's right arm was paining him from excessive use of his sword but even so he managed to knock Amrud to the ground. To deliver the death stroke he had to place the tip of his sword over Amrud's heart and lean on the other end to drive it home. Even then, Amrud, with a desperate dying effort, managed to make one final up-thrust with his short sword to pierce Murchadh's body. Although fatally wounded, Murchadh lingered until the following morning, when he received the last sacraments of his church before he died.

The Norsemen Flee

Towards the end of the day many of the Norsemen, seeing that all was lost, fled from the field towards the sea. The tide was full at the time and great numbers died in their efforts to reach their long-boats. Brodir, who had fled from the battle to Tomar wood, now emerged when he saw that the cause was lost but on his way he noticed that Brian's tent was lightly defended because most of the guard had joined in the pursuit

One fanciful account of the death of Brian Boru describes it thus:

> Brodir could see that King Brian's forces were pursuing the fugitives, and that there were only a few men left to man the wall of shields. He ran from the woods and burst through the wall of shields and hacked at the king. The boy Tadhg threw up an arm to protect Brian, but the sword cut off the arm and the king's head. The king's blood spilled over the stump of the boy's arm, and the wound healed at once. Then Brodir shouted, 'Let the word go round that Brodir has felled King Brian.'

After the battle of Clontarf the bodies of Brian Boru, his son Murchadh and those of several leading Munster chieftains were brought to Armagh. They lay in state there for twelve days and then were buried with full honours.

For many years after the Battle of Clontarf there was constant warfare between various Irish kings. In the Battle of Móin Mór near Emly, County Tipperary, between rival members of the O'Brien family of Dal Cais, County Clare, over 7,000 of the Claremen were said to have been killed.

of the fleeing Norsemen. He rushed at the remaining bodyguards and hacked his way to where Brian was kneeling in prayer with his nephew Conang. The old man and his nephew stood no chance and Brodir's axe dispatched them both. And so a day that saw a convincing victory over the invaders ended in the death of the great Irish leader.

Brodir did not escape from Clontarf, however. He and his followers concealed themselves in the nearby wood but were soon surrounded by Brian's troops and Brodir was captured alive. The annalists say he died a horrible death by having his stomach slit open and one end of his intestines tied to a tree. He was then led around the tree until death finally ended his agony.

The Burial of Brian

After the battle the bodies of Brian and Murchadh were brought to Armagh, the eclesiastical capital of Ireland, and buried with ceremony in the cathedral there. Brian's son, Donnchadh, had arrived back to Clontarf too late to take part in the battle and after the dead were buried he led the remnants of Brian's army back to Kincora.

Even though the Battle of Clontarf was not as important as the annalists later made it out to be, it did put an end to Norse raids, not only in Ireland but elsewhere as well. The Norse settlers in Ireland were left undisturbed, however, and towns like Dublin, Waterford and Wexford remained predominately Norse until the coming of the Normans in 1169 AD.

The BATTLE of DUBLIN
(September 1171)

Dermot Mac Murrough

After Rory O'Connor was crowned High King of Ireland in Dublin in 1166, among the lesser kings who submitted to him was Dermot Mac Murrough, King of Leinster. Fourteen years previous to that, Mac Murrough had abducted Dervorgilla, the wife of Tiernan O'Rourke of Breifne, while her husband was away from home. She took with her all she had brought to O'Rourke as a dowry, including 140 cows. Some historians maintain that she had arranged the whole thing!

  In 1166 the High King banished Mac Murrough from the kingdom for his continual outrageous behaviour and Mac Murrough fled to Bristol to seek help from Henry II, King of England. On learning that Henry was in France at the time Mac Murrough went to his court there and asked for help.

Dermot Mac Murrough's career was extraordinary. He was responsible for the establishment of the Priory of All Hallows on the site of present day Trinity College and also of the Augustinian Convent at nearby Hoggen Green (College Green). One of the nuns there was his own ex-wife, the sister of Archbishop Laurence O'Toole. On one occasion he attacked the town of Kildare where he dragged the abbess from her convent and married her off to one of his officers. In 1142 he attacked some of his opponents, killing two nobles, gouging out the eyes of another and blinding seventeen lesser chieftains.

At the end of her life Dervorgilla retired to the convent attached to Mellifont Abbey in County Louth. There she spent the rest of her life in prayer until she died in 1193. She is also credited with materially supporting the nuns' churches at Clonmacnoise in County Offaly.

Henry was a fierce, determined man, with great energy and ability but given to such violent rages that he was said to be possessed by the devil. He was more French than English and of his thirty-five years as King of England had spent only thirteen in the country. Henry listened to Mac Murrough and then gave him permission to go to Wales where some of Henry's toughest barons were trying to wrest as much land as they could from the Welsh.

The chief baron was Richard de Clare, Earl of Pembroke, better known as Strongbow. He had recently lost back to the rightful owners some land that his father had taken from them, so he was only too willing to listen to Mac Murrough. Strongbow agreed to come to Ireland on condition that Dermot would give him his daughter Aoife in marriage and that he would become King of Leinster on Mac Murrough's death.

Dermot Mac Murrough who invited the Normans to Ireland was afterwards known as 'Diarmaid na nGall' (Dermot of the Foreigners).

The Norman soldier was a formidable fighting man; fighting was his trade. From the age of thirteen he was specially trained for war. The most important soldiers were the mounted knights who charged the enemy in tight groups. Each knight wore a coat of mail consisting of thousands of rings of steel linked together. The head was protected by a steel helmet, the early versions being cone-shaped with a narrow strip to act as a nose guard. Later helmets covered the head completely, with slits for the eyes. Each knight carried a kite-shaped shield, usually bearing his coat of arms. For weapons they used a combination of long lances, swords, battle-axes or maces with fearsome cutting edges.

The Norman infantry did not wear armour but they did have helmets and padded tunics. The most feared of all were the archers. Mostly they used the longbow, which was about 1.8 metres in length and generally made of yew. The bowstring was made of hemp. The arrows were made of ash or oak, tipped with a steel arrowhead.

The Irish soldiers wore no protective armour at all but only wore linen tunics in battle. For weapons they had the short sword, the sling and the battle-axe.

The Normans had a well-thought-out landing drill. First on shore were the archers who took up advance positions against any attack. Not until a reconnaissance had been carried out and the all-clear given, would the men-at-arms with full equipment go ashore with their horses. They would then ride through the ranks of archers and take up the front line of assault.

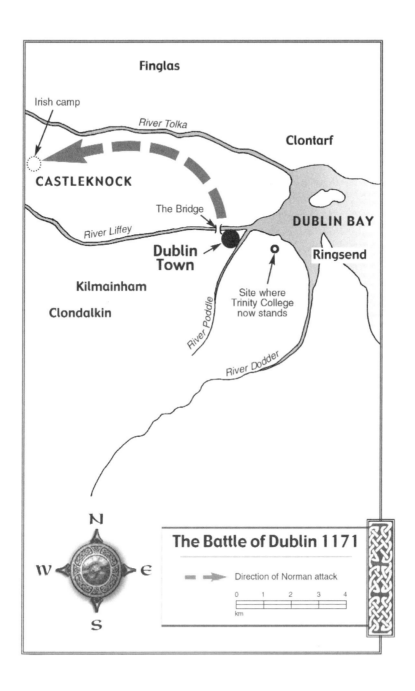

The Battle of Dublin 1171

When the Normans took over an area, instead of devastating it as the native Irish chieftains would do, they sought to consolidate their position by building a type of castle in the region.

The first fortified castles built by the Normans consisted of earthen and wooden defences called motte-and-baileys. First they built up huge circular mounds of earth over ten metres high with steep sides. On the flat top of this mound they built a wooden tower for living quarters. The whole area was then protected by a wooden palisade around the edges. A sloping ladder-like bridge connected this part, called the *motte*, to a lower area called the *bailey*. This was another circular area protected by a palisade inside which soldiers, workers, cattle, horses and provisions were kept in safety. If the castle was attacked, the people in the bailey could retire to the motte and destroy the connecting bridge.

The remains of many of these motte-and-baileys can still be seen around the country in the form of grassy mounds, without the wooden buildings of course. There were a huge number of these motte-and-baileys built in Ireland, particularly in east Ulster, Leinster and Munster, in counties such as Antrim, Louth, Dublin, Kildare, Carlow, Waterford, Tipperary and many others.

From about 1200 onwards, because the Normans were more in control in Ireland, they started to build more substantial castles of stone. The remains of many of these imposing buildings are still standing to this day in places such as Carlingford, Maynooth, Roscrea, Ferns, Nenagh and Adare.

The Coming of the Normans

The first Normans landed in Bannow Bay, County Wexford, in May 1169. The following year Strongbow arrived with 120 knights and over 1,000 archers and other foot soldiers. His army, and that of Mac Murrough, immediately attacked and captured Waterford and then, leaving a garrison in the town, marched on Dublin. The Norsemen of Dublin had a special reason for fearing the vengeance of Mac Murrough, for they had murdered his father and insultingly buried him with the body of a dog.

  The Norse King Asculph, who ruled Dublin, was prepared to resist Strongbow and asked for assistance from the High King, Rory O'Connor. O'Connor had a far larger army than the 5,000 Normans who were coming to attack Dublin, while the Wicklow Mountains presented a natural barrier to their progress. When the king arrived at the city he established his main army at Clondalkin and set up outlying defences at the Scalp above Enniskerry and at Windgates on the coast road just south of Bray. But he had not reckoned on the local knowledge of Mac Murrough, who led his army and the Normans across the mountains by way of Glendalough, Glencree and down through Rathfarnham. From there they made their way through the woods which reached to the very walls of the city. The defenders were taken by surprise and sent out Archbishop Laurence O'Toole to mediate. Long and protracted negotiations followed, during which Mac Murrough demanded that the town give him hostages and recognise him as High King. Finally the Normans lost patience and two knights, Raymond Le Gros and Milo de Cogan, rushed the town with their men and started slaughtering the townspeople. When King Asculph saw that the town was lost, he and his followers ran to some ships they

Dermot Mac Murrough altered the course of Irish history forever by his abduction of Dervorgilla. He died in 1171 and was buried in the old cathedral in Ferns, County Wexford. *The Annals of Ulster* tell of his death in these words:

> Dermot, King of the Province of Leinster, after destroying many churches and territories, died in Ferns without Extreme Unction, without Communion, without Penance, and without a Will, in reparation to Colmcille and Finian and all those saints besides whose churches he destroyed.

The walled town of Dublin was entirely on the south bank of the River Liffey, with the area now occupied by Dublin Castle in the centre. It extended as far as the River Poddle to the south, present day Parliament Street to the east, and westward to where present-day Bridge Street is now.

During Norman times oxen were very important as they were used for ploughing – their tails were tied to the plough. This practice was to last for many more centuries.

had moored in the Liffey for just such an emergency, and sailed away. O'Connor also withdrew his army and Strongbow was left in possession of Dublin.

Strongbow Declares Himself King

Early the following year Mac Murrough died and Strongbow declared himself King of Leinster. In the meantime Asculph had gathered a large army of Norse allies, amounting to about a thousand men, and set sail for Ireland to retake the town. He landed with his army where the present-day Trinity College stands and soon began laying siege to the town at its eastern gate. The Normans, as usual, were not content to wait inside the walls and they sallied out to engage Asculph's numerically superior forces. The engagement took place near present-day Dame Street, and the Normans were driven back into the town. Their leader, Milo de Cogan, then secretly sent his brother Richard, together with thirty knights, out through the west gate. Riding as fast as they could, Richard and his knights circled the walls and attacked Asculph's army at the rear. The Norsemen were taken by surprise and Richard's archers and heavy horsemen devastated their ranks. Soon those who could, fled from the battlefield and Asculph himself was taken prisoner, tried in his own palace in Dublin and immediately beheaded.

High King Besieges the City

Sometime later Rory O'Connor, the High King, arrived at Castleknock to the west of the town with a large army. Although contemporary accounts put the size of his army at 30,000 men, in all probability it was a good deal smaller. He immediately deployed his men around the city walls to blockade the town.

During Norman times there was only the most basic water supply and a complete lack of sanitary facilities in the town of Dublin. The finding of bundles of moss in excavated cesspits seems to indicate that moss was used as we would use toilet paper today. Streets were filthy and stinking from offal, carcasses and dung. Herds of scavenging pigs roamed the streets and the smells must have been horrendous. Animals grazed on the grass of Hoggen Green and other sites.

In 1224 a rudimentary water supply was provided for the city. Water was diverted from the Poddle and the Dodder along a conduit to large tanks along the High Street–Thomas Street ridge. Some pipes extended the supply from there. St Saviour's Priory, just across the Liffey to the east of the Old Bridge, had water supplied to it through a 125mm pipe. Because of the scarcity of the water supply it was decreed that 'within [the priory] the pipe is to be so narrowed that its opening may be stopped by the insertion of a man's little finger'. In houses, if they had a water supply, the pipes were to be 'no thicker than a goose quill'.

After the Norman Conquest there were constant squabbles, battles and wars between the native Irish chieftains and the new invaders and in 1263 a number of native chieftains offered the crown of Ireland to Haakon IV of Norway. Alas the king died before he could take up the offer, so we will never know what the result might have been had he done so.

The monument to Strongbow and his wife Aoife
in Dublin's Christchurch Cathedral

The siege continued for about two months with little or no fighting. The blockade soon began to have an effect and supplies inside grew so scarce that the Normans were in a desperate state. Not only could they get no help from their other Norman strongholds at Wexford and Waterford but also they had no hope of getting help from King Henry who was afraid that Strongbow might set up an independent kingdom in Ireland. By September Strongbow was finally forced to attempt a settlement with the High King. The terms offered by O'Connor were too severe for Strongbow to accept, however: the Normans could keep Dublin, Wexford and Waterford and no more; they could not have Leinster as promised by Mac Murrough, nor any other part of the island.

It was too much for the warlike Normans and they responded in character. They assembled three of their most

In 1209 one of the greatest tragedies to hit the Normans occurred in Dublin. On Easter Monday of that year a hurling match was played on a pitch located at Cullenswood, in present-day Ranelagh in Dublin. A large number of Dublin citizens were present as spectators at the match when local Irish clans attacked the proceedings. Up to 500 men were killed. This terrible tragedy, on what was called Black Monday, was commemorated annually in Dublin for 600 years. Every anniversary the colonists, fully armed and headed by a man carrying a black banner, would march out to the scene of the tragedy. There they would hold a feast and formally challenge the mountain tribes to combat.

Strongbow is buried in Christchurch Cathedral in Dublin. The original monument over the grave was destroyed by a falling wall and the present one was brought from Drogheda as a replacement. His tomb was used for centuries as a place to conclude deals, exchange documents and pay rents.

experienced units and suddenly emerged from the town at one o'clock on a September afternoon to attack O'Connor's army. The first contingent was led by Raymond le Gros, the second by Milo de Cogan, and the third by Strongbow. Each group consisted of about forty knights on horseback, sixty bowmen and 100 foot soldiers. Although the archers always operated on foot, it is thought that on this occasion they may have sat behind the riders until they were close to the enemy. It is believed that some Leinstermen and other Dublin citizens also joined the assault. In all, Strongbow seems to have had about 2,000 men.

The quickly moving force crossed the Liffey bridge and headed for Finglas. They then turned left and soon came behind the present Phoenix Park. Shortly afterwards they came on O'Connor's unsuspecting and unprepared army in Castleknock from the rear. There was complete confusion among the Irish ranks and their losses were heavy. Tradition has it that the High King was caught in his bath, although some sources say he was bathing in the Liffey, and was lucky to escape half-naked from the scene.

The slaughter continued until late afternoon and by then all the Irish troops had either fled or been killed. The siege of course was over and the triumphant Normans went back to the town with the spoils of battle and badly needed supplies for their hungry families.

The BATTLE of CLONTIBRET
(May 1595)

The Great Hugh O'Neill

Hugh O'Neill was born in Dungannon about the year 1545 and was given an English education. His first military experience was as commander of a troop of horse in the service of Queen Elizabeth I. In 1585 the Irish Parliament made him Earl of Tyrone in succession to his (reputed) grandfather, Earl Conn O'Neill, but he had been given no inheritance of the O'Neill lands which had been confiscated on the death of Shane O'Neill in 1567. Shortly afterwards he married Mabel Bagenal, sister of Marshal Henry Bagenal, who was military commander of Ireland. Bagenal had bitterly opposed the marriage and had sent his sister away to the house of another sister in Dublin. O'Neill followed her there, however, and the two were married in Drumcondra, Dublin. From that day on, Bagenal became O'Neill's deadly enemy.

Hugh O'Neill was born in Dungannon but reared in England
in the 'new religion'. He succeeded Shane O'Neill
to become the second Earl of Tyrone in 1585.

Hugh O'Neill was described by a contemporary:
> Of a medium stature but a strong body, able to
> endure labours, watching, and hard fare, being
> withal industrious and active, valiant, affable, and fit
> to manage great affairs, and of a high, dissembling,
> subtle and profound wit.

In the fifteenth and sixteenth centuries a man would be
considered lazy if he was still in bed at six o'clock in the
morning.

O'Neill became the leader of his people in 1593 and immediately set about preparing for the war with Elizabeth's army which he knew was inevitable. Notices were read out in churches and other assembly points, calling for recruits to his army, and setting out the rates of pay and other terms of service. These volunteers were known as '*buannadha*' (billeted men) and the name was later anglicised as 'bonnaghts'. They were formed into companies and were drilled and given a red uniform. They marched into battle to the sound of the drum and bagpipes and they carried battalion colours.

The War Begins

The war commenced in Ulster when Maguire of Fermanagh raided the nearby county of Monaghan but O'Neill's first act of open defiance was his attack on the queen's fort on the River Blackwater. There was a wooden bridge at the spot and the fort had been built in 1575 to protect the crossing and to act as a frontier post. The fort on the Blackwater consisted of a stone tower on the north bank of the river and an earthen fort on the Armagh side. O'Neill captured the fort and bridge and destroyed both of them in February 1595. From then on it was a war to the finish between the queen and O'Neill. O'Neill then proceeded to make sporadic attacks on various English posts in the North, including that of Monaghan. Elizabeth was forced to send supplies and reinforcements to these threatened posts under the protection of small contingents of her army. This of course gave O'Neill a great opportunity to attack her army in conditions that were entirely in his favour.

The effort to relieve Monaghan was to lead to the battle of Clontibret, six miles from Monaghan. Towards the end of May 1595, a force numbering about 1,750 men, consisting of

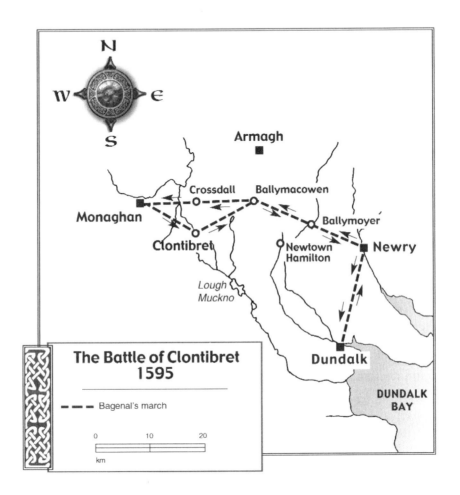

**The Battle of Clontibret
1595**

− − − − Bagenal's march

0   10   20

km

nineteen companies of infantry and six troops of horse, set out from Dundalk. It was under the command of Marshal Bagenal, O'Neill's sworn enemy. Bagenal's purpose was not an aggressive one – he was there simply to escort the convoy of supplies to the town of Monaghan, relieve its garrison and then return safely to the Pale. Bagenal reached Newry by 24 May and from there moved on towards Monaghan.

Things Don't Go Well for Bagenal

The troubles for Bagenal's army began after Newry. Because of the very boggy nature of much of the terrain between Newry and Monaghan his troops had to stick to the existing tracks or roads. When he reached Ballymoyer he decided to camp for the night. O'Neill, who had been monitoring Bagenal's progress all the time, now rode up towards the camp to examine its layout. The watching English saw him immediately and sent Sir Edward York and some horsemen towards him to parley. The two groups stood on opposite banks of the river. O'Neill is reported to have declared that by ten o'clock the next day 'it should be seen whether the queen or they should be masters of the field and owners of Ulster'.

The next day Bagenal's march resumed and proceeded without incident to the village of Crossdall, four miles from Monaghan town. O'Neill then suddenly started to attack the leading section of Bagenal's army, which contained the least experienced soldiers. Bagenal's force was marching in three separate groups of vanguard, battle and rearguard, but these were strung out over a long distance. Bagenal himself was in the rear, so the officers commanding the van did not know what to do. Eventually, a Captain Richard Cuney was chosen as leader and he ordered about 150 of his men who had firearms to lead the column. Then to their great surprise they

Two types of firearms of the time were the musket and the caliver. The caliver was the military version of the arquebus and its name was derived from French efforts to standardise the calibre of military guns. The arquebus was essentially a simple tube through which the ball moved freely, and it was highly inaccurate. The caliver, on the other hand, had a rifled barrel and consequently the bullet had a more true trajectory. The caliver weighed over five kilos and could fire a ball (or bullet), which weighed about thirty grams and had a range of less than 100 metres. Firing about thirty balls used up half a kilo of gunpowder.

The musket, which also had a rifled barrel, came originally from Spain and was longer than the caliver. It was very heavy, about 1.5 metres in length and weighed nearly ten kilos! Being so heavy it had to be fired from a rest – a portable iron fork – but it could fire eight to ten balls, each weighing sixty grams, for the expenditure of only half a kilo of gunpowder. The effective range of the musket was about 140 metres.

The musket was loaded by pouring coarse powder down the barrel, then ramming home a lead ball and a wad of rag. The gun was fired by bringing the burning end of a piece of match in contact with a small pan of fine powder on top of the barrel. The resulting flash of the powder went through the touchhole and ignited the coarse powder. (When nothing happened it was said to be 'just a flash in the pan'.) Reloading was a complicated business requiring two men to perform the operation. When a musketeer had fired he retired to the rear, reloaded and then gradually moved towards the front again.

A later development saw the invention of the flintlock which ignited the powder in the pan by means of sparks caused by a piece of flint striking against a piece of steel when the trigger was pulled.

found themselves attacked by up to 300 armed O'Neill troops clad in red coats just like English soldiers.

Nevertheless the English pressed forward, harassed from time to time by O'Neill's raiders. Bagenal, who had remained at the rear of his army, now brought his whole column forward to join Captain Cuney but O'Neill suddenly called off the fight and withdrew from the area. This tactic of alternatively attacking and retiring threw the English enemy into confusion and gave O'Neill great advantage. However, Bagenal reached Monaghan without any further difficulty, having lost, he claimed, only twelve men killed and thirty wounded, but he had used up a great deal of his precious gunpowder.

When he reached Monaghan Bagenal replaced the garrison there and started on his return journey on 27 May. It was about ten o'clock in the morning when his troops marched out, again in one column comprised of three sections as before. This time, however, Bagenal was at the head, with Sir John Chichester in the 'battle' (middle) and Cuney, together with Captain Thomas Wingfield, in the rear.

In an effort to deceive O'Neill they took a different route on the way back, but O'Neill was not easily fooled and knew exactly where they were. He brought his army to a place he knew Bagenal would pass through and there he lay in wait. The place he chose was Clontibret near the borders of Counties Armagh and Monaghan.

The Start of the Battle

Late in the afternoon, when he was about five kilometres from Monaghan town, Bagenal saw the Irish army in the distance, but he continued his march to Clontibret. When Bagenal's army was in an open and flat plain with 'a bog on

A common weapon of the time was the pike. It was a long staff of about four metres and usually made of ash. It had a sharp metal tip at the end. The strongest men in the company carried the pikes and as they marched forward they carried them horizontally at shoulder height with the tips slanted downwards. When attacked by cavalry, the pikemen would form a square with the butts of their pikes grounded and the tips raised to form the famous infantry 'hedgehog'.

Bows and arrows were no longer used by English troops toward the end of Queen Elizabeth's reign but O'Neill used Scottish archers against Bagenal at Clontibret.

Primitive cannon guns called 'bombards' were invented in the fifteenth century and these could fire enormous stones for long distances. One, the 'great mortar of Moscow' had a bore measuring ninety centimetres and could fire a stone projectile weighing a tonne. By the sixteenth century the guns had become so massive that they required twenty-five horses to pull them.

The defeat at Clontibret had a profound effect on the ordinary government troops. One company of Cheshiremen, who had fought in the battle and were later ordered to march to Connacht, started the march 100 strong but only sixteen reached their destination. The rest simply deserted.

every side', O'Neill began his attack. Once again Captain Cuney was unlucky: he and his raw soldiers were in the rear where O'Neill concentrated his attack this time.

Once the battle started O'Neill never let up for seven or eight hours. He first of all raked the sides of the enemy column with fusillades of shots and then attacked in force at its rear. He used both horse and foot very skilfully in accordance with the best military tactics of the time. His horse soldiers led the infantry forward, but they were protected in front by a formation of soldiers with firearms who kept firing all the time as quickly as they could. In this way the Irish were able to get close to the English ranks, well within range of the deadly javelins hurled by the attacking Irish cavalry. Bagenal sent his own cavalry against the attackers but could do little against the larger forces of O'Neill with their muskets and calivers, backed up by old-fashioned mercenary Scottish archers.

Although the action was spread over a long distance it was at Clontibret that the most decisive incident took place. The path ran through a bog and O'Neill blocked the pass and held and pounded the enemy for over three hours. The English ammunition ran very low and their pikemen began to waver 'for lack of shot to save them'.

At this moment O'Neill could be seen sitting on his horse in full view of the enemy, 'surveying the battle and giving his orders', with his cavalry in formation behind him. In a last desperate effort, Seagrave, a gigantic officer from the Pale, spurred his horse across the river and charged at O'Neill. Each man broke his horseman's staff on the corselet of the other and then Seagrave threw himself onto O'Neill. The two men fell to the ground where Seagrave's enormous strength was slowly crushing O'Neill to death. The quick action of one of O'Neill's men in cutting off one of Seagrave's arms undoubtedly saved the earl's life. O'Neill then killed Seagrave with his dagger.

Eventually the English column forced their way slowly forward, being harassed by O'Neill whenever the terrain suited him. Casualties mounted among the English, with some 109 of their officers and men being wounded and thirty-one killed. (O'Neill later claimed to have killed and wounded up to 700 men, while the English authorities admitted that there were 'more hurt in the late service than was convenient to declare'.) They had been marching all day and now at late afternoon their officers decided that they had to halt for the night. They found a suitable 'non-boggy' site at Ballymacowen and when they checked their military supplies they found that they had only 150 grams of powder per piece left. This would allow only about three rounds for a musket or maybe ten for a caliver. Their ammunition was desperately short also, so Bagenal's and Chichester's pewter dishes were melted down to make bullets. They also sent a messenger to Newry with frantic appeals for more ammunition.

Although the English did not know it, O'Neill was in an even worse plight. He had used up all his ammunition, having burned 650 kilos of powder compared with Bagenal's 450 kilos. O'Neill now also sent an urgent request for more to his castle at Dungannon.

The next day Bagenal's column renewed its march and in the evening they entered Newry 'wearied and hungry'. They never knew how near they had been to disaster and that they had only survived because of O'Neill's empty ammunition bags. Bagenal told his superiors that he dared not march to Dundalk because of O'Neill who was lying in wait in the Moyry pass.

Powder now arrived by sea for Bagenal and with it came the

final humiliation with the order that he and his foot soldiers should return to Dublin by sea and that his horse should remain in Newry. Elizabeth later 'spoke bitterly of the dishonour that she had been made to suffer'.

By 6 June Bagenal was in Drogheda, having sent all his wounded back to Dublin on the ships. The whole episode had been a disaster for the English and one of great encouragement for O'Neill.

The BATTLE of the YELLOW FORD
(October 1598)

Hugh O'Neill Prepares

The government proclaimed Hugh O'Neill a traitor in June 1595 and shortly later a garrison was installed in Armagh cathedral. O'Neill feared that his stronghold at Dungannon would soon be attacked and responded by breaking it down and hiding its contents at secret locations on the many islands on the Tyrone lakes. For the rest of the year the government forces were continually harassed by O'Neill and suffered heavy losses as they endeavoured to bring supplies to the Armagh garrison.

Because the Lord Deputy, Sir William Russell, could make no headway against O'Neill he was glad to enter into what was intended as a brief truce but in fact it continued from the end of 1595 to the summer of 1597.

In May 1597 a new Lord Deputy, Lord Thomas Burgh, was

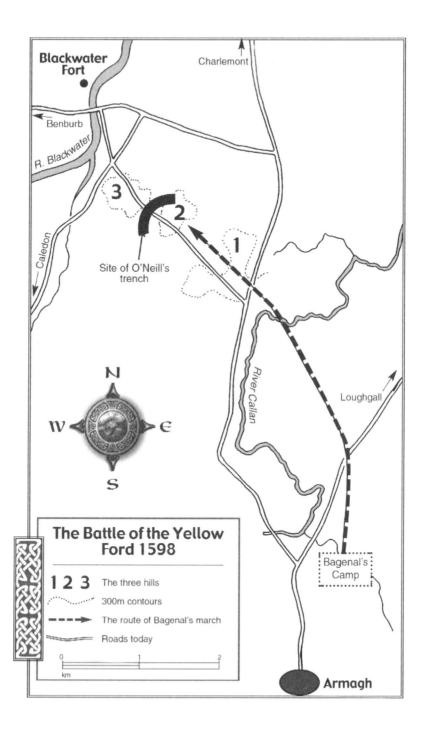

Blackwater
Fort

Charlemont

Benburb

R. Blackwater

Caledon

3

2

1

Site of O'Neill's
trench

River Callan

Loughgall

N

W   E

S

The Battle of the Yellow
Ford 1598

1 2 3   The three hills

....   300m contours

- - - ▶   The route of Bagenal's march

≈≈≈≈   Roads today

0   1   2
km

Bagenal's
Camp

Armagh

appointed. He was a real 'go-getter' and a keen fighter. He gathered a force of about 3,500 men and marched his army at speed as far as Armagh by 13 July. He soon arrived at the Blackwater but for eight whole weeks could move no further because O'Neill barred his way. He then contented himself by rebuilding the fort, which had been destroyed by O'Neill, on the northern bank of the river.

The fort on the Blackwater was a very rough earthwork construction, just a parapet behind a ditch, protecting an enclosure around a flat oblong area. Burgh garrisoned the fort with 150 men under the command of Captain Thomas Williams. The defences were soon tested but Williams managed to beat off the Irish attack. O'Neill's men did not entirely withdraw, however, but remained close by and blockaded the fort. O'Neill then sought to gain more time and negotiated another truce which lasted till the following summer.

O'Neill was in a very strong position: he knew that Queen Elizabeth would be reluctant to mount another expensive campaign against him where he held all the advantages. By 1598 O'Neill and his allies had about 6,000 *bonnaghts* billeted throughout Ulster. These men were so well trained by Spanish and Irish officers that the English officers were amazed at their proficiency. They said that O'Neill's men were 'as ready, well disciplined and as good marksmen as France, Flanders or Spain can show'. By this time every able-bodied man in O'Neill's territory, without distinction of class, was trained in the use of weapons. Not only that, but his forces could be assembled from the most remote parts in just three days. The English, on the other hand, needed three weeks to do the same.

The truce between O'Neill and the Irish Council ended in

June 1598. Initially the council wanted to give up the fort as it was more trouble than it was worth but the availability of more troops, the fear of the queen's disapproval, and the eagerness of Marshal Bagenal to try to avenge his defeat by his brother-in-law and personal enemy, O'Neill, at Clontibret, led to another attempt to defeat the Northern leader.

Bagenal Leads His Forces North

Bagenal was given the command and he assembled a force of about 4,000 foot and 300 horse. Nearly half his men were Irish, while the rest were composed of Englishmen and some soldiers from Brittany. A large number of his force were raw recruits who were almost unmanageable – they fought continually among themselves, sold their uniforms and arms for drinking money, and deserted freely. Bagenal's horse troops, many of whom were Irish, were old hands, however.

The various elements of his army assembled in Ardee on 7 August and from there they marched to Armagh. They brought four cannon guns with them – the heaviest of which was a 'saker' – pulled by a team of oxen. (A saker was a small cannon much used at the time during sieges and on ships.) On the morning of 14 August the army set out for the River Blackwater with the objective of relieving the fort there.

Bagenal knew that O'Neill would attempt to block his progress and in fact he could see his enemy's men 'upon the highway betwixt us and the Blackwater, on the other side of the pass and the River Callan which we were to pass the next day'. Bagenal hoped that he could avoid the most dangerous spots by leaving the highway and marching across country on mostly hard ground except for a bog he hoped to make passable by means of boughs and sticks carried by his army.

His column stretched for about two kilometres from

beginning to end, with six regiments of 500 men each, with nearly 100-metre gaps between them. In these spaces were his cavalry, guns, spare horses and packhorses laden with supplies for the fort and the material to make the bog passable. Marshal Bagenal was in charge of the vanguard regiments and some veterans of Clontibret, such as Cuney, Wingfield and others, were in charge of the rear. Waiting for them was O'Neill, Red Hugh O'Donnell of Donegal, and Hugh Maguire of Fermanagh, with an army of more than 5,000 men.

The route taken by Bagenal's army is known but details are missing. The route required the crossing of several small hills, a cornfield and bogs, in the middle of which was the so-called 'yellow ford'.

O'Neill was well aware of the route they were taking and had plenty of time to make preparations. He dug a deep trench, extending for over half a mile between two bogs and cornfield, directly across the route Bagenal was taking. He also 'plashed' the shrubbery in the area, that is, he bent down and interwove the branches to form an impenetrable barrier to both men and horses.

Bagenal Under Constant Attack

The first regiments of Bagenal's column, led by Colonel Sir Richard Percy, set out on the march northwards and were continually attacked in the flanks by O'Neill's men. He had also to halt several times so as not to get too far ahead of Bagenal's own regiment. Percy pushed on, however, crossed the Callan river, went over a small hill, then the 'yellow ford' in the bog, and on to the top of a second small hill. He then marched his men down to a field of green corn surrounded by another bog and finally to the top of a third small hill. He

The Earl of Ormond, the commander of the queen's forces in Ireland, said it would be better 'if the scurvy fort at Blackwater had never been built'.

The 'Yellow Ford' cannot be identified with any certainty. It may not have been a river crossing at all, but a place where a yellowish-coloured water flowed from the bogs, hence the name. It is believed to be in the townland of Tulligoonigan.

One of Colonel Percy's Welsh ensigns, Evan Owen, when he saw that the battle was lost, wrapped himself in the company's colours 'which were heavy and new' and decorated with silver crescents, the Percy emblem. He was soon cut to pieces for refusing to give up the colours.

A large number of colours were lost by the English troops in the battles. Every captain of a company had his own colours and there were forty companies in Bagenal's army.

waited there for Bagenal to catch up with him. He was so far ahead of the rest of the column he could see William's garrison marching out of the fort with colours flying. When the garrison saw Percy's English colours they 'threw up their caps for joy, hoping to have a better supper than the dinner they had that day'.

Bagenal and the main body of his army was quite a distance behind Percy – in fact there was such a gap between the various regiments that communication between them completely broke down. The saker was proving to be quite a handicap too. It kept sinking in the boggy ground and large teams of men were required to pull it free on many occasions. In fact when it got to the ford it stuck so fast that Wingfield, who was in charge of the gun, considered abandoning it.

About this time Bagenal decided to retreat and sent orders on ahead to Percy and others to retire. Percy was in great difficulty when Bagenal's order reached him but he made desperate efforts to obey. The way back was very hazardous, as his rearguard was being vigorously attacked by O'Neill and soon his whole force were fighting for their lives.

It was in the middle of this chaos that the cry went up that Bagenal was dead. The brave marshal had fought in the thick of battle but when he raised his visor to survey the situation and take a breath, a carefully aimed musket ball pierced his brain and he fell dead.

The news of Bagenal's death so affected Percy's men that the retreat turned into a rout – discipline broke down in the regiment and it was 'driven in great disorder over the trenches, tumbling one over another'. Percy himself was hit by a gunshot in his breast plate and knocked to the ground but was pulled to safety by his Irish horseboy.

Wingfield took command after Bagenal's death and resumed efforts to organise the retreat to Armagh. The ill-fated saker stuck fast again and had to be abandoned as a wheel was broken and all the oxen were killed. To add to the chaos, many of his men were killed by a tremendous explosion which occurred when a soldier went to an open barrel of gunpowder to refill his flask. He accidentally touched the powder with his lighted match, causing not only that barrel to explode but another one close by as well.

Most of the English column continued its desperate efforts to retreat, while some regiments attempted to move forward. There was complete confusion in their ranks and all the time they were being attacked by O'Neill.

The battle had been in progress for nearly four hours and it was now early in the afternoon. The retreat continued with the rear squadron of horse protecting the regiments carrying the body of their slain leader. As they approached the ford they saw O'Neill's men also making towards it 'with the colours flying which was taken from the vanguard of all, minding to make good the ford before us'. The English troops, led by Captain Richard Billings, got there first, however, and held it for the retreating troops to get through.

Wingfield had meanwhile gathered as many survivors as he could find and brought them all to the ford. He then sent Captain Billings' regiment ahead to clear the way to Armagh and followed behind with all that remained of the force. They eventually reached Armagh too and set about fortifying the cathedral as their headquarters. Over 2,000 English troops reached Armagh and eventually Dublin.

At the end of that eventful day the English had lost twenty-five officers, 800 soldiers killed and over 400 wounded. Many of the English troops fled and were never accounted for. Over 300 men went over to O'Neill's side and at the end of it all the Blackwater fort had to be surrendered. The Irish are said to have lost about 200 killed and 600 wounded.

The BATTLE of KINSALE
(December 1601)

'Spanish Ale Shall Give You Hope'

Following requests from Hugh O'Neill and Red Hugh O'Donnell for aid in their continued war against the English, 3,500 Spanish troops under the command of Don Juan Del Aguila, landed at Kinsale, thirteen miles south of Cork, on 21 September 1601.

Lord Deputy Mountjoy responded immediately and by 27 September had brought his army to Cork. He ordered that every soldier in Munster, apart from the Waterford garrison, should join him against the Spanish invaders. The response was so good that by 14 October he had about 14,000 soldiers under his command, and to service such a large force, he demanded, and received, supplies from England.

The weapons of O'Neill's army were as up-to-date as they could make them. They had matchlock muskets, calivers, fowling pieces, swords, helmets, pikes, powder and shot. Most of this material came from Spain.

The abbreviated signature of Red Hugh O'Donnell in Irish.

Hugh O'Neill's signature on a document in 1601.

Before sailing to Ireland to aid O'Neill and O'Donnell the Spanish considered four possible landing places: Donegal, East Ulster, North Leinster and the southwest of Ireland. In the end they opted for Kinsale in the southwest because a landing there could more easily be reinforced, there was a readily available food supply and the surrounding countryside was level and suitable for manoeuvre.

In 1599 O'Neill got seven and a half tons of gunpowder, a thousand arquebuses, a thousand pikes, five tons of lead, and a large quantity of match; in 1600 he got a further thousand arquebuses; in 1601 another similar cargo arrived. Of course, pikes were also manufactured at home, but these were given to standby men such as shepherds; the Spanish pikes went to his best forces.

O'Neill gave presents of guns to anyone who showed an aptitude in their use and one observer said, 'even the farmers, ploughmen, swineherds, shepherds, and very boys have learned to use this weapon.' The Lord Deputy Mountjoy even said that they were better trained and disciplined than the government troops.

Within a few days of the Spanish arrival, O'Neill got letters from the commander, Del Aguila, calling on him to join him. True to form, however, O'Neill took his time to make up his mind about the action he should take and even towards the end of November, Mountjoy's spies were telling him that O'Neill would never bring his army south. O'Neill's apparent lack of response may just have been a tactic to keep his enemies guessing, for he immediately set about organising his army in a quiet way and making sure that his territory would be secure in his absence.

By October O'Neill set up camp at Lough Ramor in Cavan and had an army of up to 2,000 foot and 500 horse by month's end. Then on 9 November 1601 he led his army south, with Maguire of Fermanagh, O'Reilly of Breifne (Leitrim-Cavan) and other Northern leaders, under his command. Again he kept the spies guessing by travelling only at night, with each soldier carrying his own military supply of powder and shot, and a food supply of butter and meal.

Hugh O'Donnell, meanwhile, had his own troubles in

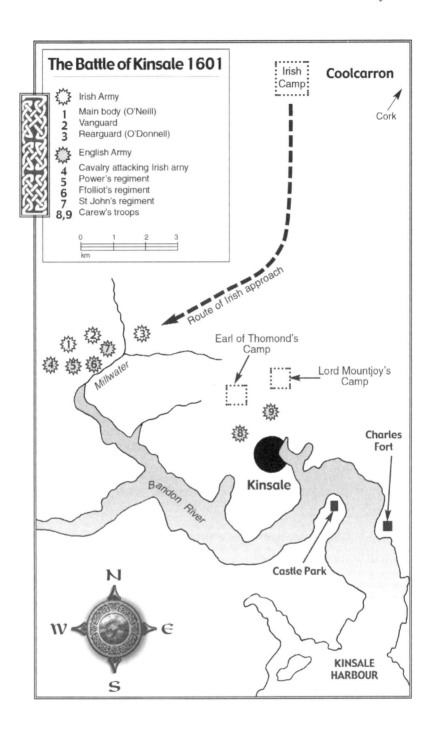

The Battle of Kinsale 1601

Irish Army

1 Main body (O'Neill)
2 Vanguard
3 Rearguard (O'Donnell)

English Army

4 Cavalry attacking Irish arny
5 Power's regiment
6 Ffolliot's regiment
7 St John's regiment
8,9 Carew's troops

0 1 2 3
km

Irish Camp
Coolcarron

Cork

Route of Irish approach

Earl of Thomond's Camp

Lord Mountjoy's Camp

Millwater

Bandon River

Kinsale

Charles Fort

Castle Park

KINSALE HARBOUR

N
W E
S

Donegal with a cousin, Niall Garbh O'Donnell, who had attacked some of Hugh's strongholds. In fact when the call to Kinsale came, O'Donnell was attacking Niall in Donegal town. The Lord Deputy's spies also said that O'Donnell would not go south but he confounded them by gathering his army in Ballymote, County Sligo, and marching for Kinsale on 2 November.

As they marched they collected more men on the way and when they reached Roscrea in Tipperary they had a total of about 2,000 foot and 300 horse. Here O'Donnell waited impatiently for O'Neill to join him and was said to have been very annoyed at the delay.

'The Longest Winter March'

Sir George Carew, the President of Munster, lost no time however, and brought an army of about 2,500 men to block O'Donnell's path to Kinsale. The weather at the time was extremely wintry and an intense frost on the night of 22 November froze rivers and bogs. O'Donnell took advantage of the frozen ground to cross the Slieve Felim mountains and march down into Cork. The sixty-kilometre march amazed Carew, who called it 'the greatest march with encumbrance of carriage that hath been heard of'. O'Neill eventually joined O'Donnell at Bandon on 21 December and then the combined strength of the two armies was about 5,000 men.

Meanwhile Del Aguila, who had originally taken both Charles Fort and Castle Park outside the town of Kinsale, was now inside with an army of over 3,000 men. He was an energetic and active general and had made several sorties outside the wall to attack the enemy forces. These forces under Carew and Mountjoy numbered about 7,500 men. (On paper they were supposed to have had many more but quite a large number of the men were laid low with illness.) The English forces formed a barrier between the town and the approaching Irish armies and they also attempted various assaults on the town's defences from time to time. By December, however, Mountjoy's forces became increasingly affected by illness, so he had his men dig trenches and then settled down to a blockade.

On 21 December the Irish forces encamped at Coolcarron just north of the town of Kinsale. By this time their overall strength had grown by a further 500 Munstermen and about 200 additional Spanish soldiers who had arrived by ship in Castlehaven on 21 December.

O'Donnell was getting more and more impatient to commence the attack but the ever cautious O'Neill said that all the Irish forces had to do was wait and that a great number of the enemy would die 'owing to contagion and sickness'. O'Donnell's viewpoint seems to have prevailed, however, and the battle commenced on Christmas Eve with the march of their whole forces towards Kinsale. Mountjoy had prior knowledge of the Irish plans through his spies (another version is that an Irish traitor named Brian Mac Mahon sent him the information) and had established a special regiment of men under Sir Henry Power to quickly respond to any emergency.

Meanwhile the Irish army had marched southwards towards Kinsale and then changed direction to bring them to the northwest of the town. Some reports say that the Irish troops lost their way in the darkness, while others say there was a dispute between O'Neill and O'Donnell as to who would lead the van. At any rate, when dawn broke many of their troops were strung out quite a distance behind by the time the vanguard came in sight of the town. O'Neill's troops were the first to approach and they then halted to prepare their muskets and light their match. The foremost English scouts soon noticed the lights in the still-dark morning and raised the alarm. Mountjoy responded extremely quickly. He ordered his men to arms and he and Sir Richard Wingfield rode forward to observe the situation for themselves.

Mountjoy had already decided on his tactics: five infantry regiments under Carew were to remain in his camp, and four regiments would stay in the Earl of Thomond's camp. These forces were to act as a reserve and to withstand any attack from the Spanish troops. Three other regiments led by officers Power, Ffolliat and St-John were to confront the Irish forces. Carew had about 5,000 under his command, while Mountjoy had about 2000 foot and 400 horse.

The Battle Begins

Meanwhile O'Neill's men were still halted, perhaps because O'Donnell had not yet caught up with them or perhaps O'Neill was reacting with his usual caution. Whatever the reason, he had lost the initiative. Mountjoy ordered an immediate attack and, as O'Neill's men withdrew across a stream to firmer ground, they were under continuous fire from the English troops. Attempts by cavalry and musketeers from Mountjoy's army to force a way across did not succeed, so that he was obliged to seek another way to where O'Neill had halted. Mountjoy discovered a passage over boggy ground and Wingfield led a cavalry charge against the main body of Irish troops. At the crucial moment, however, they wheeled away rather than charge the well-prepared Irish troops, who jeered the perceived lack of courage on the part of the cavalry.

O'Neill was still in a strong position – his army had firm

ground under them and the enemy would have a bog behind them if they attacked, while his experienced skirmishers were as effective as ever.

Mountjoy by now had all his cavalry together, except those with Carew in front of Kinsale. O'Neill's horse were lighter and not used to dealing with a full frontal charge, so that when such a charge by Mountjoy's cavalry now took place, the Irish horse fled from the field. In their mad rush to get away they overran the positions of their own foot soldiers. Mountjoy then attacked O'Neill's main body of troops. Already disorganised by the fleeing horsemen, the troops put up little resistance and Mountjoy's men were able to kill and slaughter at will. First the troops at the rear gave way and soon it turned into a complete rout – the day was lost. A short while later Del Aguila surrendered the town and, giving up any strongholds held by his forces, returned to Spain, while the broken Irish armies retired to Innishannon.

The SIEGE of DUNBOY
and the Retreat O'Sullivan Beare
(1602)

Shortly after the battle at Kinsale the Spanish leader, Del Aguila, meekly surrendered the town of Kinsale and also castles at Dunboy, Baltimore and Castlehaven which had garrisons of Spanish troops. He then sailed for Spain where he was arrested for his failure in Ireland and this so affected him that he died of grief a short time later.

Meanwhile the Irish chieftains had taken their broken armies to Innishannon where they held a council of war. It was decided that Red Hugh O'Donnell should go immediately to Spain to seek further help. Having appointed his brother Rory as commander of the Donegal troops, he slowly made his way to Spain. King Philip received him with great courtesy, and promised to send another, even stronger expedition than Del Aguila's with him when he returned to Ireland. Unfortunately Red Hugh never saw Ireland again as he died suddenly at the early age of twenty-nine on 10 September 1602.

When the Irish chieftains heard of Del Aguila's surrender of the castles they were extremely angry and the owner of Dunboy, Donal O'Sullivan Beare, chief of Beare and Bantry, determined to recover his castle before it was handed over to Sir George Carew, President of Munster. Marching quickly back to Dunboy, which was situated on a tip of the mainland jutting into the sea-channel just west of Great Beare Island, O'Sullivan sent away the Spanish garrison and installed his own men, under the command of Richard Mac Geoghegan and Thomas Taylor, an Englishman. The little garrison – it numbered only 143 men – immediately set about strengthening the castle's defences.

Carew, meantime, had set out from Cork with an army of 3,000 men to take over from the departing Spanish, sending his cannon and stores on ahead on board ship. When he arrived at Bantry he was joined by another 1,000 men under Sir Charles Wilmot and the combined forces then proceeded by ship to Great Beare Island. They arrived in early June 1602 and set up camp within sight of Dunboy castle.

Carew wasted no time in calling for the surrender of the castle and, on being peremptorily refused, started the siege with a fierce bombardment with his cannon. The unrelenting assault continued for days and by 17 June the walls were so shattered that Mac Geoghegan sent a messenger to Carew with an offer to surrender, provided the garrison would be allowed to march away with their weapons. Carew's reply was to hang the messenger and to order an even more ferocious assault by cannon, and by sending a storming party to the breach.

Although the gallant band of defenders fought with extraordinary courage, they were eventually driven back bit by bit to the relatively unscathed eastern wing. The only approach to this part of the castle was through a narrow passage and a furious hand-to-hand battle now took place there for an hour and a half. Other defenders poured a hail of bullets, stones, and every kind of material to hand, on the attackers.

While this fierce encounter was going on, a party of the besiegers had accidently discovered a hidden entrance into the castle and now attacked the defenders from the rear. The fierce fighting continued until forty of the garrison sallied forth in a desperate effort to escape to the Great Beare Island. Before they even reached the shore however, they were cut down and killed, all except eight who managed to plunge into the sea. Carew had stationed soldiers in some boats for just such an eventuality, and in his own words, 'had the killing of them all'. The attack on the castle had lasted all day, and by evening Dunboy lay in ruins and its garrison much reduced in number. Finally there were only seventy-seven defenders left and they were forced to take refuge in the castle's cellars. Carew's attacking army then halted their attack until morning as they knew that the defenders could go nowhere in the meantime.

The next morning Carew resumed the siege with a fusillade against the cellars. Most of the weary defenders, with Taylor in command (for Mac Geoghegan was mortally wounded) were determined to fight to the death but twenty-three of them laid down their arms and surrendered. Carew then ordered his cannon to fire directly at the cellars and they caused such destruction that Taylor's men at last begged him to surrender and he did so.

A party of Carew's soldiers then entered the cellars to take the defenders captive and as they did so, the mortally

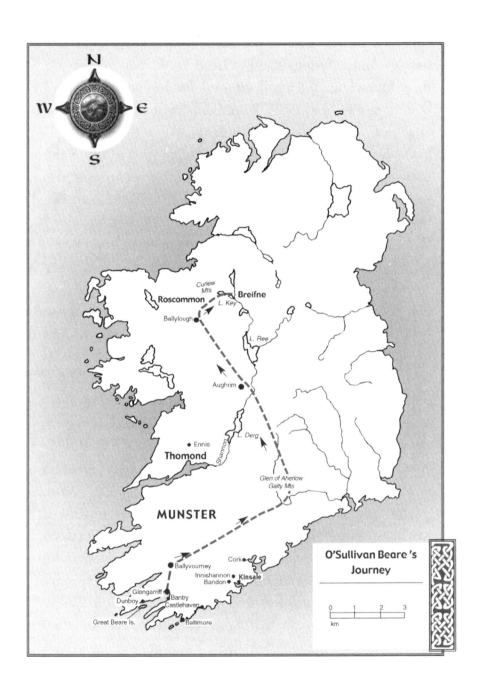

O'Sullivan Beare's Journey

wounded Mac Geoghegan snatched a lighted candle from Taylor's hand and attempted to reach some barrels of gunpowder in the corner of the cellar. He never reached them, however, as one of Carew's officers caught hold of him and held him in his arms while Carew's soldiers killed him with their swords.

Later Carew executed fifty-eight of the men who had surrendered and endeavoured to extract information from Taylor and fourteen others by promising to let them go free, but they refused and were all hanged.

O'Sullivan Beare

As a final act, all the gunpowder in the castle was gathered in the vaults, a fuse was set, and the whole lot exploded with such devastating effect that nothing was left standing of Dunboy but two side walls.

Other castles belonging to Donal O'Sullivan Beare had been captured earlier and now, with the loss of Dunboy, he had no castle left. He still had a small determined fighting force in the Glengarriff area and for a while he continued the battle against the forces of the Crown. Then towards the end of 1602 he got the terrible news that Red Hugh O'Donnell was dead and that the promised aid from King Philip had been cancelled. He knew then that he would never be secure in Munster, so he decided to march north to Breifne (Leitrim-Cavan) to seek refuge there. On 31 December 1602 he set out from Glengarriff at the head of 400 soldiers and 600 other men, women and children on the long march north.

They had not time to prepare properly for their journey and were only able to gather sufficient food for one day, but as O'Sullivan had received plenty of money from Spain he hoped to obtain food and provisions along the way.

They were beset by enemies every step of the way and they suffered continually from cold, hunger and fatigue. The famous Irish chroniclers, the Four Masters, wrote,

> O'Sullivan was not a day or night during this period without a battle, or being vehemently or vindictively pursued, all which he sustained and responded to with manliness and vigour.

The people in the areas through which they passed were so terrified of the vengeance of Carew that they would not sell food or goods to O'Sullivan's little army so that his men had to steal supplies or take them by force. This was resisted by the inhabitants of course and the small army suffered losses nearly every day. Some members of the group fell behind or could go no further, some died from wounds or fatigue, and others were killed in fighting.

Their first day's march of twenty-four hours took them over the mountains as far as Ballyvourney. The next day brought them through Duhallow and on to Liscarroll where they had to cross a ford. They were attacked by the local chief there and lost four of their men. On they went till they came to the Glen of Aherlow but could get no food or drink except herbs and water.

By now they were so weary that the very sentries had great difficulty in staying awake at night. In their journey up to this they had erected tents each night but now they were not even able to do this and were forced to sleep under the open skies.

From the Galtees they made their way across Tipperary, beset on every side by enemies, so that they had to be under the constant protection of the fighting men while a detachment sought food and provisions from the countryside.

It was at this stage in the journey that O'Sullivan's wife was forced to make a painful decision. She had borne the trials and hardships of the journey without complaining, even though she was carrying her two-year-old son, but now for his sake she had to part with him. She gave him to one of her most trusted lady-servants with the request that she should care for him as her own. (This the lady did most faithfully, caring for the child until it was safe to send him to join his parents in Spain some time later.) O'Sullivan's wife did not complete the journey but she did survive and joined her husband later.

On the ninth day of their march O'Sullivan and his little band reached Portland near the Shannon in north Tipperary. At this stage the broad Shannon lay before them while enemies were still close behind them. There were no boats that they could use and no ford that they could cross on foot, but fortunately one of the men was a skilled maker of currachs (wickerwork boats covered with animal hides). Under his instructions they made boat frames from boughs and reeds, tied together with make-shift ropes. They then killed twelve of their horses and covered the curraghs with the hides. (The horsemeat was carefully kept for food.)

Hurriedly clambering aboard their boats, the little band took it in turns to cross the river. In the middle of this operation a local chieftain, named Donagh Mac Egan, started to attack the men and attempted to throw women and children into the Shannon. O'Sullivan remonstrated with him in vain, so he turned on Mac Egan and killed him.

Crossing the Shannon did not end their worries and as they marched northwards they had to fight their way through ambush after ambush. By this time most of the horses carrying the sick and wounded had gone lame, so that O'Sullivan had to make the heart-rending decision to leave behind those who could not walk.

The desperate band pressed onwards with the despairing cries of their comrades ringing in their ears. Eventually O'Sullivan and his little band approached Aughrim in County Galway and were here confronted by Captain Henry Malbie with a force greater than their own. O'Sullivan had one advantage, however: a soft boggy piece of ground lay directly in front between him and the attackers. He gave instructions to his men to protect the rear and sides in order to lure Malbie to attack across the bog, and as he did so O'Sullivan gave the counter-attack order. Malbie was shot dead immediately and his demoralised men soon gave way before the desperate and furious onslaught of O'Sullivan's men.

The next part of their journey took them through the territory of local chief, Mac David Burke, who harassed them at every step. When they reached Ballinlough in County Roscommon they sought to take shelter for the night in a thick wood but a friendly sympathiser warned them that Mac David Burke intended to surround the wood and attack them when daylight came. So on they marched through the night in dreadful conditions of rain, sleet and snow. When morning came they discovered that Mac David Burke was close behind but when he approached them, he was so put off by their determination to resist any attack that he withdrew from the area.

Their path next took them across the Curlew Mountains to Knockvicar beside Lough Key and here they considered it safe enough to rest for a while. The next morning a local guide pointed out the towers of O'Rourke's Breifne Castle in the distance. That same morning at eleven o'clock O'Sullivan and his weary followers entered the castle to a warm welcome from the owner.

They had set out, a thousand strong, from Glengarriff a fortnight before but only Donal O'Sullivan, seventeen armed men, sixteen servants, and the wife of O'Sullivan's uncle, Dermot – thirty-five in all – had completed the journey that day. Over the next few days small groups of twos and threes arrived to join the survivors but all the rest had either died or decided to start a new life in the communities along the way.

O'Sullivan Beare's signature, 1601:
'Yours most faythfull and bounden, Don. OSulyvan Beare'

The BATTLE of BENBURB
(June 1646)

The Plantation of Ulster

Although the Irish soldiers suffered a humiliating defeat in open battle at Kinsale, another Irish army more than erased their shame forty-five years later when they fought at Benburb, County Tyrone in 1646.

After Kinsale the Plantation of Ulster was carried out whereby the native landowners were dispossessed and their lands given to English and Scottish settlers. During the succeeding years the native population in Ulster – the Old Irish – was treated very badly by Lord Deputy Mountjoy and his successor, Arthur Chichester, while the Anglo-Irish gentry of the Leinster Pale, all Catholics and all loyal, were treated with extreme harshness by the Lords Justices, Sir William Parsons and Sir John Borlase.

Finally some of the Old Irish leaders, among whom were

Rory O'More of Laois, Sir Phelim O'Neill of Tyrone, Lord Maguire of Fermanagh, and Hugh Óg McMahon of Oriel (Monaghan-Armagh), held meetings and decided that their only hope of redress lay in insurrection. They hoped to get help from Europe, particularly from Owen Roe O'Neill, a nephew of the great Hugh O'Neill, who had distinguished himself in the army of Spain. He had expressed a great willingness to join their cause and had urged an immediate insurrection.

Owen Roe O'Neill defeated a Scottish army led by General Monro
in the Battle of Benburb, June 1646.

The leaders settled on 23 October 1641 as the day of action when they would seize Dublin Castle but the evening before a man named Owen Connolly, to whom McMahon had confided the secret, went to Parsons and told him of the plot. The authorities immediately arrested all the plotters they could find and so stymied the plans for Dublin. The rising went ahead in Ulster, however, and very soon nearly all Ulster was in the hands of the rebels who were commanded by Sir Phelim O'Neill. In many cases the pent-up fury of years was released against the planters, many of whom were driven from their homesteads and their goods plundered. Many were also killed.

The successes in Ulster inspired others and by the end of the year the rebellion had spread throughout the whole country.

Four Parties with Four Armies

At the beginning of 1642 there were four distinct parties in Ireland, each of whom had an army.

First: The Old Irish led by Rory O'More aimed at total separation from England. Their army was mostly in Ulster under the command of Sir Phelim O'Neill.

Second: The Anglo-Irish Catholics representing the rest of Ireland's Catholics wanted freedom of religion but not complete separation from England.

(The Old Irish and the Anglo-Irish didn't really trust each other.)

Third: The Puritans (or Parliamentarians), under the Scottish General, Robert Monro, who were mostly confined to Ulster.

Fourth: The Royalists who held Dublin were mostly Protestants of the Established Church and opposed the Parliamentarians.

The war ebbed and flowed during the early part of 1642. Sometimes the rebels were successful and sometimes the Parliamentarians were. Gradually the Parliamentary forces began to get the upper hand in Ulster, particularly, because the leader of the rebels, Sir Phelim O'Neill, had no military experience. Monro's Scottish troops numbered nearly 20,000 men and they were able to plunder and massacre at will. The rebels sent urgent requests for assistance from Owen Roe O'Neill and he responded by arriving on a single ship with

150 or 200 veterans of the Irish-Spanish regiments, some of them officers, in Donegal in July 1642. He also brought some carbines and gunpowder. Owen Roe immediately took charge and started re-organising the Irish troops. He imposed strict discipline, released all Protestant prisoners and punished severely any offenders guilty of cruelty or plunder.

Colonel Thomas Preston Lands with 500 Men

Another Irish-Spanish officer, Colonel Thomas Preston, landed in Wexford soon afterwards with 500 men and stores. Preston, brother of Lord Gormanstown, had distinguished himself in wars in Europe. A priest who knew both men said of Owen Roe that he was a 'man of great prudence and conduct, very adroit and crafty in the handling of great matters'. Preston, on the other hand was 'very brave but not a man of much prudence', although he was more popular with his men than Owen Roe was with his. Preston was given command of the Anglo-Irish Catholic army.

The two branches supporting the Catholic cause were often at loggerheads with each other and in 1642 the bishops made a determined effort to get them to act in concert. To this end a special general assembly of the leaders of both factions was held in Kilkenny on 24 October, 1642. After proclaiming their loyalty to King Charles I, the 'Confederation of Kilkenny' assumed the right to govern the country for the time being. It appointed O'Neill as general of the army in Ulster and Preston over the army in Leinster.

The arrangement seemed to work well in the beginning and the two generals pursued the war in their respective areas of command with some success. Gradually, however, a bitter rivalry developed between the two men – Preston hated O'Neill and O'Neill made no effort to hide his contempt for Preston.

The Pope Sends an Emissary with Aid

In 1645 the Pope sent over John Baptist Rinuccini, Archbishop of Fermo in Italy, with a large supply of arms for the Catholic cause. He brought 2,000 muskets (mostly matchlocks), 2,000 boxes of bullets, 4,000 swords, 2,000 pike heads, 400 pairs of pistols and a large supply of gunpowder and match. Although most of these supplies eventually went to Owen Roe in Ulster, the Anglo-Irish party delayed their delivery as long as possible.

With the money from Rinuccini, O'Neill gathered an army of 5,000 foot and 500 horse in the spring of 1645 and established his camp on the Hill of Gallanagh near Lough Sheelin in County Cavan. He immediately set about a rigorous training programme for his men, so that before long he had a powerful disciplined force equal to anything he had had in Europe.

The initial moves towards war started in 1645 when General Robert Monro began to march south. His objective was to carry the war into the confederation's territory and maybe take Kilkenny as well. He had over 6,000 men, 600 horse and six field guns pulled by oxen. He intended meeting up with another force from Coleraine, led by his son-in-law, Colonel George Monro. This force had 100 horse and 240 musketeers, while a third force of 2,000 men, led by Sir Robert Stewart, was coming from the Foyle Valley. The two Monro contingents were to make towards Kilkenny, while Stewart's force was to proceed to Connacht and join the Parliamentary leader there, Sir Charles Coote.

When O'Neill discovered Monro's plans he broke up camp and led his men northwards to intercept him. O'Neill went through Cavan and Monaghan and reached Glaslough, west of Armagh, on 3 June, 1646. The next morning he marched

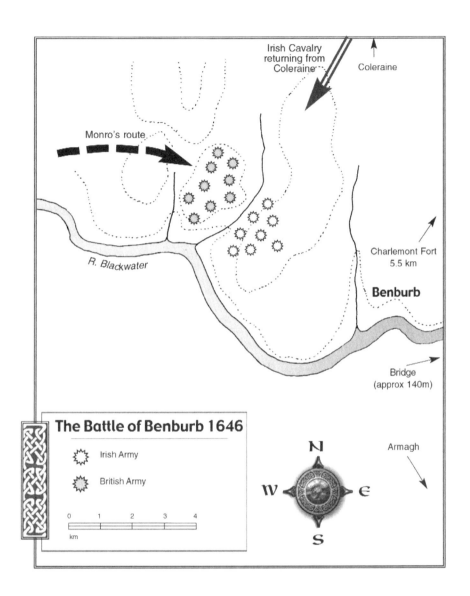

Irish Cavalry returning from Coleraine

Coleraine

Monro's route

Charlemont Fort
5.5 km

R. Blackwater

Benburb

Bridge
(approx 140m)

The Battle of Benburb 1646

Irish Army

British Army

0   1   2   3   4
km

N

W   E

S

Armagh

to the valley of the Blackwater, and camped with his whole army on the north bank of the river at Benburb. At Armagh, General Monro's spies, in turn, had told him of O'Neill's intentions and he turned aside from his course to crush O'Neill's army and marched for Glaslough also.

On 5 June O'Neill sent out two regiments to intercept George Monro and set about selecting the most favourable position at Benburb for the coming battle. He chose an excellent site between two small hills, with a wood to his rear. He divided his army into seven sections, placing four of them to the front with wide spaces between them and the other three slightly behind so that they could take the places of any of the other four if required during the battle.

Meanwhile General Robert Monro had been told by a captured Irish soldier that O'Neill was marching to Benburb with a force of about 6,000 troops and Monro thought it was an opportunity not to be missed of crushing O'Neill once and for all. He marched his army at all speed towards Benburb and by 4 June had reached Armagh. The next morning he made a personal trip towards Benburb to see what the situation was like there. He saw at once that his only hope of crossing the Blackwater without much loss of troops was at Caledon, five miles from Benburb. This would also have the added advantage of catching O'Neill's army between his own force and that of Colonel George Monro coming from Coleraine. Once across the river he turned his army towards Benburb. O'Neill's spies kept him well informed of General Monro's moves and immediately sent most of his cavalry and a small force of foot, under Lieutenant Colonel Brian Roe O'Neill, to halt the advance of George Monro. He then waited for the enemy's main army.

Owen Roe O'Neill's recruits were attracted by the pay of three shillings and sixpence a week, when Preston's men only got two shillings and sixpence.

The Irish infantrymen wore no armour but some had an iron or steel 'bowl-like' cap under their hats to protect them from sword slashes. They called this cap the 'secret'.

Sir Phelim O'Neill took possession of Charlemont Fort on the River Blackwater, Mountjoy's strongpoint of 1602, by a clever trick. He showed the garrison commander a commission, with the royal seal attached, which he said he had got from King Charles I, and was given command of the fort. The whole document was a forgery and he had found the seal in one of the castles.

General Robert Monro, commander of the Parliamentarians, escaped after the Battle of Benburb by throwing away his topcoat, helmet and wig, and mingling with the rest of the fleeing soldiers.

The Battle Begins

On the morning of 5 June 1646 General Monro organised his troops, much like O'Neill had done, into nine divisions with five in front and four behind. (It turned out that the spaces between the front divisions were too narrow to permit the rear divisions to move up.)

As Monro's army advanced towards the Irish position, O'Neill sent a detachment to halt the advancing columns but the Scottish artillery quickly routed the Irish troops. Soon the two armies stood within sight of each other but O'Neill knew that Monro's troops were tired after their long march and kept them continually on the alert by the traditional light skirmishes until late evening. By this time the sun was shining straight in the faces of the Scottish army but Monro's hopes were raised when he saw what he took to be George Monro's troops returning to his aid. When it became clear that this body of troops was in fact O'Neill's two regiments, Monro became alarmed and ordered the retreat.

Owen Roe reacted immediately, moving his three rear divisions into the gaps in the first ranks to form a continuous line. He gave the order to attack and the whole army surged forward with sword and pike. Monro attempted to halt the attackers by sending his cavalry against them but these were driven back. He then ordered the rear infantry divisions forward but found that the gaps he had left were too narrow. During the ensuing confusion, with the sun shining straight in the faces of the Scottish army, O'Neill's well-ordered battalions fell on them. Monro's army was completely overwhelmed and turned and rushed back in complete rout. The deep Blackwater River lay in their path and huge numbers were drowned in their attempts to cross. In fact so many were drowned that it is said that most who succeeded in crossing did so by walking on the bodies piled in the water.

Over 2,000 Scottish troops were killed and Monro himself was forced to flee in panic. O'Neill's losses in killed and wounded is reckoned at no more than 200.

Owen Roe's victory at Benburb was quite as brilliant as that of his uncle Hugh O'Neill at the Yellow Ford in 1598 and was the only pitched battle that Irish forces ever won.

The BATTLE of RATHMINES
(August 1649)

Dublin, the Ultimate Prize

The ultimate success of the Cromwellian campaign in Ireland in the seventeenth century depended on the capture of Dublin. Some years earlier the plotters of the rebellion in 1641 had attempted to seize Dublin Castle at the very outset. Their failure to do so meant the whole enterprise was doomed to failure. Likewise, if the forces of Owen Roe O'Neill and Colonel Thomas Preston could have taken the city after the victory at Benburb, the subsequent failures could have been avoided.

Dublin at the time was held for the Royalist cause by James Butler, later Duke of Ormond, and when he was eventually forced by circumstances to give it up in June 1647, he tamely handed it over to the English Parliamentarians, rather than to O'Neill or Preston. As he said at the time 'he preferred the English rebels to Irish ones'.

A contemporary account of Preston was that he suffered
from constant indigestion – he was 'delicate in his diet'. He
was a man 'wavering in his resolutions, imperious in his
commands and fiery in his deportment'.

Colonel Michael Jones, commander of the Parliamentary
army, was described by a contemporary as 'an uncouth and
austere fanatic, but a very brave and brilliant soldier'.

The Parliamentary chroniclers said of the battle at
Dungan's Hill:

> This was the most signal victory with the greatest loss
> to the rebels that ever was gained in Ireland since the
> first conquest thereof by the English. For which make
> us truly thankful.

Preston's campaign got off to a poor start when he was decisively defeated in 1647 by Colonel Michael Jones, the commander of the Parliamentary army, at Dungan's Hill, near Trim in County Meath. Ormond's surrender of Dublin to the Parliamentarians had also included Trim, Navan, Naas, Drogheda and Dundalk, and Preston had laid siege to Trim in an attempt to win it back. On 1 August Jones led an army of about 4,000 infantry and 800 cavalry towards the town to raise the siege. Other forces of about 700 cavalry and 1,200 infantry came from Drogheda, Dundalk and Down to join him. Preston, who had an army of about 1,000 horse and 7,000 foot, immediately vacated his position at Trim and crossed the Boyne to Portlester in County Meath.

Later, while Jones was occupied in Trim, Preston decided to March to Dublin in the hope of getting there before the Parliamentarians knew he had gone. Jones, however, learned of the manoeuvre and sent 500 horse to watch his progress and, noticing that Preston was moving at a very leisurely pace, set out with his army to follow him. When Preston became aware that Jones was closing behind, he decided to make a stand at Dungan's Hill, southeast of Summerhill in County Meath. In the subsequent battle Preston suffered a comprehensive defeat, losing nearly 5,000 men and all his guns. Another severe loss was that of all of his oxen, which were used in pulling the cannon.

Ormond Returns from England

After handing over Dublin to the Parliamentarians in June 1647, Ormond had gone to England and now he returned to lead a force of Royalists to recover the city which he had so tamely surrendered. In June 1649 he led a Royalist army of 5,000 foot and 1,500 horse to camp at Finglas on the northern side of the city. The following month the towns of Dundalk, Drogheda, Trim and Newry surrendered to Ormond's ally, Murrough O'Brien (Lord Inchiquin). O'Brien then joined Ormond at Finglas with a further 4,000 men. Even with this large army, Ormond thought he could not take the city by force, so he decided on a blockade to starve Jones out. Leaving 2,500 men in Finglas, he brought the rest of his army to Rathmines, where he encamped about two miles from the city in the area occupied by the present-day Palmerston Park. If Ormond had hoped to take the city with ease, that hope quickly faded when further reinforcements for Jones arrived on the Liffey on 26 July, 1649. The extra 2,000 foot and 600 horse brought Jones' army up to almost equal strength with Ormond. Adding further to Ormond's discomfort were strong rumours, carefully spread by Jones, that Cromwell himself was at Bristol, preparing to land in Munster. Ormond's position was not helped either by his distrust of some of his erstwhile enemies, such as Preston and Inchiquin, who now commanded sections of his army. He was given conflicting advice on the best tactics to adopt: some wanted him to withdraw to Drogheda and other safe havens until events unfolded, others were afraid that Jones might come between their camp and their troops on the north side of the Liffey and advised that Ormond should move from Rathmines to Drimnagh. A sort of compromise was decided on – they should take Rathfarnham Castle, held by the Parliamentarians, to protect their rear. This was done on 28 July and, encouraged by this success, Ormond decided to bring his army down along the River Dodder, through Donnybrook and on towards Ringsend. This would have the dual advantage of cutting Jones off from valuable grazing fields around Baggot Street and also would deny entry of reinforcements to Jones by sea.

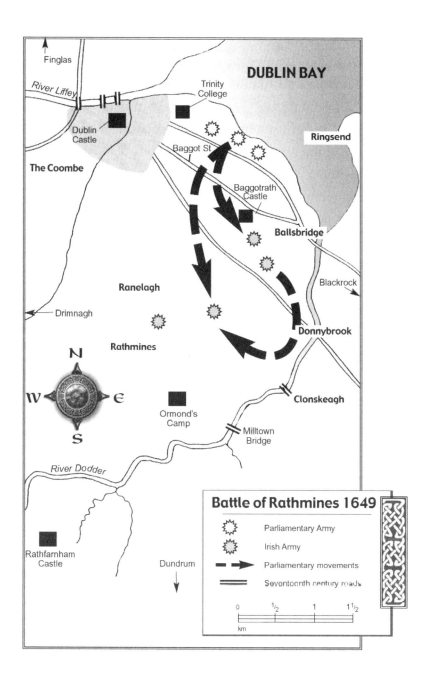

Finglas

River Liffey

DUBLIN BAY

Trinity
College

Dublin
Castle

The Coombe

Baggot St

Ringsend

Baggotrath
Castle

Ballsbridge

Ranelagh

Blackrock

Drimnagh

Rathmines

Donnybrook

N

W   E

S

Ormond's
Camp

Clonskeagh

Milltown
Bridge

River Dodder

Rathfarnham
Castle

Dundrum

Battle of Rathmines 1649

Parliamentary Army

Irish Army

Parliamentary movements

Seventeenth century roads

0   ½   1   1½

km

Baggotrath Castle Under Attack

To achieve these aims, the possession of Baggotrath Castle, situated where the present day Baggot Street Bridge stands, was vital. Jones also knew that, so he tried to demolish the castle but only partially succeeded. Ormond's officers were convinced that they could restore it enough to make it a strong position, so he sent a force of 1,500 foot and 800 sappers under the command of Major General Purcell to attack and repair the castle after midnight on 2 August. Another force of cavalry under Sir William Vaughan, who was ordered to join Purcell, arrived at the castle early in the morning.

Strangely enough, it had taken Purcell a number of hours to cover the mile distance to the castle and when Ormond rode down to the castle the following morning he found that Purcell had only just arrived and had not yet organised the castle's defences. He had also failed to surprise Jones, who had become aware of Purcell's approach and had discreetly withdrawn from his path.

Ormond was then faced with the dilemma of either holding on to Baggotrath Castle and risking the inevitable attack from Jones, or withdrawing his garrison and leaving the castle to the enemy. In the end he decided that the best choice would be to hold the castle for as long as possible. He told his commanders that it was vital to hold the castle as it posed a threat to Jones and gave instructions on the positions to be taken up by Purcell's foot soldiers and Vaughan's cavalry. Ormond knew that an attack could come at any moment but was so exhausted that he withdrew to his tent to sleep.

The Parliamentary commander, however, did not sleep. He led his forces of over a thousand cavalry and nearly 4,000 infantry across the fields between the city and where the present-day canal is situated. Once in position at the castle, he launched an immediate attack. Vaughan's cavalry were utterly routed and Vaughan himself was killed. Purcell's infantry held out for a while longer but in the end they too were overrun. By ten o'clock the battle was over – Baggotrath Castle was in Jones' hands.

The Battle of Rathmines

Meanwhile, Ormond had barely fallen asleep before being awakened by the noise of battle. He hastily mounted his horse and rode back towards the castle to see the situation for himself. He was appalled by what he saw and rushed back to the main body of his own army, which was under Colonel Gifford and was stationed in the Rathmines area. He placed a regiment commanded by his brother, Colonel Richard Butler, and another under Colonel Myles O'Reilly, to his right and told them to remain there until they received further orders. Jones advanced steadily in the meantime, capturing positions and cannon guns on his way. Another section of his troops had reached Milltown and, turning back towards the west, had arrived behind Ormond and Gifford. (It seemed that the regiments commanded by Myles O'Reilly and Richard Butler, for want of specific orders, had left their positions for areas, where, in their opinion, their assistance was more urgently needed.)

Jones' men were strongly resisted by Gifford's troops for a while but then another body of Parliamentary horse and foot managed to circle around behind them and Gifford's men became surrounded. Feeling their situation to be hopeless, the men willingly accepted the good terms offered to surrender. Not only that, being mostly English, they agreed to join their fellow countrymen in the service of the Parliament.

Before the battle at Rathmines began, Jones had actively started the rumour that Oliver Cromwell had landed in Dublin Bay during the night with all his forces and was on his way to Rathmines. So great was the fear of Cromwell in Royalist hearts that many of them threw down their arms and ran away.

Jones claimed to have killed 4,000 men at Rathmines but as that was the total number of Royalists who opposed him, the admission by the Irish that they lost 600 men is more likely to be true.

Cannonballs and musket shot continually being dug up in modern times shows that the battle of Rathmines must have continued along a good stretch of the River Dodder.

After the battle a wounded horse wandered into a tavern near Portobello and the tavern owner later named his premises The Bleeding Horse, a name that has lasted to the present day.

When Cromwell was told of the good news from Rathmines he wrote on 13 August, 1649,

> This is an astonishing mercy; so great and seasonable as indeed we are like them that dreamed. What can we say! The Lord hath filled our souls with thankfulness, that our mouths may be full of His praise – and in our lives too; and grant that we never forget His goodness to us. These things seem to strengthen our faith and love against more difficult times. Sir, pray for me, that I may walk worthy of the Lord in all that He hath called me unto.

Ormond's situation was now hopeless and when he reconnoitred around his troops' positions he found that his units were disintegrating everywhere. After a battle which lasted no more than two hours, Jones now controlled the whole area south of the Liffey. The Royalists to the north of the river, under Lord Dillon, soon knew of Ormond's defeat and retired to Trim and Drogheda.

The SIEGE of DROGHEDA
(September 1649)

Cromwell Arrives

Shortly after the defeat of the Royalist forces in England by the Parliamentarians, the Parliamentary leader, Oliver Cromwell, turned his attention to Ireland. He arrived on the Liffey in Dublin on 15 August, 1649, and was welcomed by the citizens with open arms. A week later Cromwell issued a proclamation which was posted up on every available surface throughout the area controlled by the authorities. The proclamation condemned all acts of robbery, pillage and cruelty by his troops and announced that all offenders would be punished, irrespective of rank. It promised fair taxation and that all provisions required by the army would be paid for.

After consultation with his parliamentary commander, Colonel Michael Jones, and his son-in-law, Henry Ireton, Cromwell decided to bring his army north to attack

Oliver Cromwell was a gentleman farmer from the east of England, who had no military training but emerged as the greatest general of the English Civil War. He believed everything he had heard about the massacre of Protestants during the rising of 1641 and perhaps this explains the appalling harshness with which he treated Irish Catholics later.

According to reports Cromwell was violently seasick during the crossing from England to Ireland.

Among Cromwell's supplies when he came to Ireland were thousands of bibles, which were to be distributed among his soldiers and to the native Irish (who would not understand a word of their contents!).

Oliver Cromwell

Drogheda which was the key to Ulster. He had chosen twelve regiments of 'stout and resolute' men for the task of taking the town. Because the transport of his army's heavy cannons was slow and cumbersome, he decided to have them carried by ship to the mouth of the Boyne.

Cromwell Sets Out for Drogheda

On 31 August 1649 the army assembled at Collinstown north of Dublin and then set off on the thirty-mile march to Drogheda. As the troops slowly made their way northwards, two of the men decided to steal some hens from a local woman. When Cromwell was informed of this breach of his proclamation he promptly had the two troopers hanged as an example to the rest.

On 2 September Cromwell's army approached through the fields of Bryanstown, just south of the town of Drogheda. He then prepared the sites for his artillery pieces which were coming by sea, but due to strong winds the ships carrying the guns were delayed and did not arrive until 5 September at the Boyne. It took until Sunday, 9 September, before they were all in place.

During this period of delay Cromwell again demonstrated his insistence that his troops behave in a fair manner by having three men shot on the Friday, and a further two hanged on the Saturday, for stealing from the locals.

Meanwhile the garrison and inhabitants of Drogheda set about improving their defences. The Royalist commander, Sir Arthur Aston, was a brave and capable man who had fought with distinction in the English Civil War. He had also served in Russia under the Swedish king, Gustavus Adolphus, and in Poland under Sigismund, King of Poland. One of his contemporaries wrote at the time concerning him '. . . there

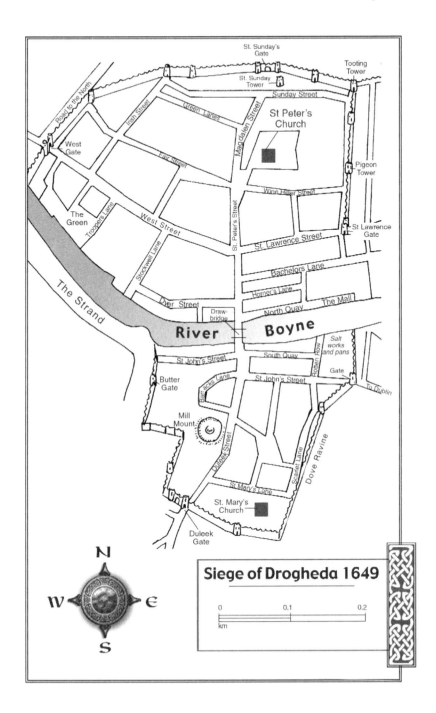

Siege of Drogheda 1649

is not in the King's army a man of greater reputation or one of whom the enemy had greater dread.' However he had an unfortunate accident in England, breaking his leg in a fall from his horse and when gangrene set in his leg had to be amputated. A wooden leg was substituted and he soon bravely overcame his disability.

The ancient town of Drogheda was built about three miles from the mouth of the Boyne and on both sides of the river. A bridge across the river had a gatehouse and a drawbridge, so that the loss of one side of the town would not necessarily lead to the loss of the whole town. Another prominent feature was the Mill Mount on the south side, a large earthwork with a strong masonry tower on top.

Aston organised long trenches to be dug inside and outside the southern walls with a view to impeding the coming attack. The trenches would not be manned and the soil dug out was piled high behind them. His troops were ill prepared to repel an attack, however, as they were very poorly equipped for the task before them. But even so, there was confidence among the Royalists that Drogheda could withstand a siege. It was hoped that 'Colonel Hunger and Major Sickness' would decimate the ranks of the attackers. With a garrison of 3,000 and with the protection of the town's high strong walls Aston was sure he could resist any attack.

As a preliminary tactic Aston ordered frequent sudden sallies out through the main gates against the besiegers but these gained him little advantage. In fact he lost quite a number of his men, up to seven per cent of his army, in these futile sorties.

The Siege Begins

On Monday 10 September 1649 a note from Oliver Cromwell was delivered to Governor Aston. The note said:

A week before the siege began, Sir Arthur Aston, the Royalist Commander, wrote:

> Yesternight theer came heether from Dundalke ten barrels of pouther, but very little match and that is a thinge moste wanting heer; and for round shote, not any at all. I beseech your Excellency bee pleased to give speedy orders for sum, as also for the sudden coming of men and monies. Belly food I perceive, will prove scarce amongst us, but my endeavours shall never be sparing to approve myself.

A Cromwellian account published at the time, 12 October, 1649, says that after Mill Mount:

> our horse and foot followed them [the fleeing defenders] so fast over the bridge which goes over a broad river, it being very long and houses on both sides, yet they had not time to pull up the drawbridge. There our men fell violently in upon them, and I believe there was above 2,000 put to the sword. We had about twenty or thirty men slain and some forty wounded. Their governor was killed in the first onset.

After Cromwell's forces captured Drogheda many of the leading ladies of the town were found hiding in a church's crypt, but they too were killed without mercy. One officer wrote later of finding 'the flower and choicest of the women and ladies of the town' among whom was 'a handsome virgin, arrayed in costly and gorgeous apparel, who knelt before him with tears and prayers to save her life'. He took pity on her and raised her up but another soldier thrust his sword through her body. Whereupon her erstwhile rescuer threw her down, having first taken all her money and jewellery.

Sir,

Having brought the army belonging to the Parliament of England before this place to reduce it to obedience, to the end effusion of blood may be prevented, I thought fit to summon you to deliver the same into my hands to their use. If this be refused you will have no cause to blame me.

Aston immediately followed the instructions of the town council and refused to surrender. The refusal brought an immediate response: Cromwell ordered his artillery to open fire. His gunners concentrated their fire on the spire of St Mary's church, which was just inside the southernmost wall. The steeple had been used as an observation post by Aston and he had positioned some mortars lower down. Cromwell's guns proved to be out of range of the mortars, however, and very soon the church had to be abandoned.

Next Cromwell's fire was concentrated on the area between Duleek Gate and St Mary's Church and by noon the following day had fired 200 to 300 cannonballs into the walls. Gaping holes were soon made in the town walls and the church, and the bombardment continued throughout the day.

By the evening of 11 September Cromwell decided that the breaches in the wall were sufficient to attempt an assault. Three regiments under Colonel Ewer, Colonel Hewson and Colonel Castle were ordered to attack. Colonel Castle was immediately shot in the head and died on the spot. After some heavy fighting the attackers retreated but were rallied by their officers and resumed the attack. Again they were repulsed and Cromwell, who was watching, was so exasperated that he rushed to the breach and called on the reserves to follow him. This time the assault was successful. Colonel Wall, the officer

Among the slain at Drogheda was Sir Edmund Verney, Aston's second-in-comand. His brother received the following letter shortly afterwards: 'Your brother Sir Edmund Verney – who behaved himself with the greatest gallantry that could be – he was slain at Drogheda three days after quarter was given him as he was walking with Cromwell by way of protection. One Ropier . . . called him aside in a pretence to speak with him, being formerly of acquaintance, and instead of some friendly office which Sir Edmund might expect from him, he barbarously ran him through with a tuck; but I am confident to see this act revenged.

'The next day after, one Lieutenant Colonel Boyle, who had quarter likewise given to him, as he was at dinner with my Lady More . . . one of Cromwell's soldiers came and whispered in his ear to tell him that he must presently be put to death who, rising from the table, the lady asked whither he was going. He answered, 'Madam to die', who no sooner stepped out of the room but he was shot to death. These are cruelties of those traitors who, no doubt, will find the like mercy when they stand in need of it.'

Various figures have been given for the total numbers killed in Drogheda but some reports claim that more than 2,500 out of the garrison of 3,100 were killed and several hundred of the inhabitants lost their lives.

commanding the defenders at the breach, was killed and the Cromwellians surged through the opening.

The death of Colonel Wall caused panic among many of the defenders and they turned and ran for the drawbridge over the Boyne two hundred metres away. They were unable to raise the drawbridge because they were so hotly pursued by their attackers, and both the fleeing soldiers and their pursuers crossed over.

Mill Mount, the earthwork inside of which Sir Arthur Aston and 250 of his defenders were positioned, was now surrounded by the inrushing soldiers. A Cromwellian officer, Lieutenant Colonel Axtell, and twelve of his men climbed to the top of the mount and demanded the surrender of those inside. At first they refused but eventually agreed to climb up to the windmill at the top of the mount and laid down their arms. They were immediately slaughtered on the direct orders of Cromwell himself.

It was widely believed that Aston's wooden leg was hollow and filled with gold sovereigns, so when the soldiers captured him they wrenched off his leg. When they discovered that the leg was only solid wood they were so infuriated that they beat him to death with it. His leather belt was found to contain 200 gold sovereigns, however, and the soldiers divided these among themselves.

Meanwhile many of the defending officers and men who had fled over the bridge to the north side of the river had taken refuge in St Peter's Church at the top of St Peter's Street. When Cromwell led his army to this spot he called on the Royalists to surrender but they refused. Then in his own words:

> . . . I ordered the steeple of St Peter's Church to be
> fired, when one of them was heard to say in the midst

of the flames, 'God damn me, God confound me, I
burn, I burn.'

The account tells of how Colonel Hewson put three barrels
of powder into the church and blew them up. This only
damaged the body of the church and later that night he had
the church seats broken up and placed in a great pile under
the steeple. When the pile was set alight it quickly set fire to
the lofts above and soon the church bells, the roof and the
men came all crashing down together.

Two towers in the town, one at St Sunday's gate and one at
West Gate were still occupied by the Royalists. The round
tower near St Sunday's Gate near the north wall of the town
had about 130 men sheltering there. When they refused to
surrender Cromwell posted a guard all around it to prevent
any escape and to starve the garrison into submission. The
defenders kept shooting at their attackers and killed some of
them. Cromwell then ordered an assault on the tower and
forced the garrison to surrender. Then in Cromwell's words:

> The officers were knocked on the head and every tenth
> man of the soldiers killed and the rest shipped to the
> Barbadoes. The soldiers in the other tower were all
> spared, as to their lives only, and shipped likewise to the
> Barbadoes.

The SIEGE of CLONMEL
(April 1650)

Cromwell Moves On to Clonmel

After the capture of Drogheda other towns in the northern half of the country, such as Dundalk, Carlingford, Newry and Trim, quickly surrendered. Cromwell then moved south and took Wexford, Cork and various other Munster towns with little opposition.

The town of Clonmel in Tipperary put up a stiff resistance, however. The defence of the town was in the capable hands of another member of the famous O'Neill clan of Ulster. He was Hugh Dubh (Black Hugh) O'Neill, a nephew of Owen Roe and was about fifty years old at the time.

He was quite an experienced soldier, having spent sixteen years in the service of Owen Roe in Europe. He had been actively involved with his uncle in the siege of Arras on the frontier between Spain and France and the experience

Cromwellian Soldier

gained there was to stand him in good stead in Clonmel. In 1649 he had been appointed governor of Clonmel by the Lord Lieutenant, Ormond.

The garrison in Clonmel included 1,500 Ulster infantry, mainly from Cavan and Tyrone, and 100 cavalry under a Major Fennell. Although 400 reinforcements were sent in response to earnest pleas to Ormond for assistance, they arrived too late to help. The local townspeople, led by the mayor, John White, also actively assisted in the preparation of the defences.

On Saturday 27 April 1650 Cromwell and his army appeared at the north side of Clonmel. His call to the garrison to surrender was rejected by Hugh Dubh who said he had no intention of delivering up the town and dared Cromwell to do his worst.

The Siege Begins

Cromwell set his guns on Gallows Hill overlooking the town and launched successive assaults on the walls but none was successful. O'Neill did not sit quietly waiting for the worst to happen but organised highly successful sorties from the town against what he perceived to be the weakest positions of the Ironside attackers. Before the Cromwellians would have time to recover, O'Neill's men would have retired to the safety of the town's wall. It is estimated that Cromwell may have lost up to 500 of his men in these attacks. The story goes that Cromwell now tried a different tactic and in some way had arranged a deal with Major Fennell by which, on the payment of £500, Cromwell's troops would be allowed into the town unopposed. Hugh Dubh, however, did not fully trust his subordinate and decided to inspect his defences one night. When he found that one gate in the walls was defended solely

Owen Roe died in November 1649 in Cavan as he was on his way to confront Cromwell. He was in poor health for quite a while beforehand and rumours that he had been poisoned seem to have no foundation. He is buried inside the Franciscan church there, of which nothing remains today but the tower.

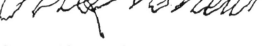

Signature of Owen Roe O'Neill shortly before his death.

Roger Boyle (Lord Broghill) had gone into exile in London, having supported Charles I earlier in the war. He then decided to travel to Holland, where Prince Charles was lying low at the time, and get a commission to raise a Munster army for the Royalist cause. Cromwell got wind of Broghill's intentions and asked him to come to see him. Broghill was astonished that Cromwell even knew of his existence and, full of curiosity, went to meet him. When Cromwell then told him that he knew of his plan to raise an army for Charles he thought that he was going to be arrested. Instead Cromwell asked him to switch allegiance to the Parliamentary side and Broghill promptly did so!

by Fennell's men he immediately dismissed them and replaced them with his own troops. As pre-arranged by Fennell, about 500 Cromwellian soldiers were admitted through the gate and once inside were immediately slaughtered by Hugh Dubh's men.

Cromwell's besieging army was then strengthened by more troops from his new friend, Lord Broghill. Although Cromwell's guns could not force a surrender, they were still able to breach the walls sufficiently in one place to warrant an assault by his troops. Hugh Dubh had anticipated the attack, however, and under the cover of darkness he had his men and the townspeople construct a long lane of mud, stones and timber that stretched from the breach into the town, and at the end of the lane they dug a large ditch. Two cannon were concealed above the ditch overlooking the lane and directly opposite the hole in the wall. These cannon were loaded with chain-shot to cause the greatest havoc on the attacking infantry.

The next morning on 17 May Cromwell ordered the attack. There was no opposition and his troops poured into the makeshift lane. When the leaders reached the ditch at the end they shouted 'Halt! Halt!' but those behind took it to be directed at fleeing defenders and, with cries of 'Advance! Advance!' more than 1,000 of the attackers crowded into the narrow space. And then O'Neill struck. His men took control of the breach in the wall and allowed no further attackers in nor those inside to get out. The two hidden cannon opened fire, while the defenders alongside the lane poured volley after volley on the trapped Cromwellians. There was such terrible carnage that none survived.

In vain did Cromwell try to get his infantry to resume the attack but then two cavalry colonels, Langley and Sankey,

During the siege of Clonmel one attack was led by Colonel Charles Langley but as he tried to climb over the defences his hand was cut off by a scythe. He survived however and was granted lands at Ballingarry, County Tipperary. He later had a steel replacement hand made, and the hand is said to have remained in the family until the early twentieth century.

Cromwell's health was generally bad during his time spent in Ireland. He now nominated his son-in-law, Henry Ireton, as his successor and got ready to leave for England. On 29 May 1650 he went aboard a frigate called *The President* and sailed for England after nine months spent in Ireland. This had been his first trip abroad and he never again left England.

agreed to lead their regiments on foot to renew the attack. They surged towards the breach and, though they did manage to penetrate the defences, they fared no better inside than the previous hapless attackers. Even though Cromwell threw more and more troops into the attack Hugh Dubh was more than capable of dealing with them. Hundreds of Ironsides were cut down and eventually Cromwell was forced to order his troops to withdraw.

Cromwell on the Point of Withdrawing

Legend has it that Cromwell was on the point of abandoning the siege altogether when one of his men discovered that a bullet fired from the town was made of silver. This implied that O'Neill was desperately short of lead for use in his men's guns and was reduced to using every available metal in the town as ammunition. This fact encouraged Cromwell to continue the siege, for he knew the town would eventually have to give in.

That night a delegation from the town, led by John White, came out to negotiate a settlement. Cromwell was eager to agree and the two sides signed the surrender terms. It was only then that Cromwell thought to ask if Hugh Dubh O'Neill backed the surrender. He was said to be furious to learn that O'Neill and his men had sneaked out of the town while the negotiations were going on. In spite of his anger, however, he honoured his agreement and treated the inhabitants in a civilised manner.

The SIEGE of DERRY
(1689)

Northern Disasters and Atrocities

While the massacres which followed Cromwell's taking of Drogheda were to forever live in the memories of Irish nationalists the northern colonists of Derry had the events of 1641 to stiffen their resistance a generation later.

One writer on the 1641 rebellion had put the numbers of Protestants killed in the first two or three days at forty to fifty thousand. Another said it was 150,000 in two months. Another increased it to 200,000. The actual figure was in fact something between 4,000 and 6,000.

Even more horrifying for the colonists were the stories of atrocities such as at Portadown when 'the Protestants in multitudes were forced over the bridge whereby at several times they were drowned in the River Bann above one thousand'. At Loughgall 300 Protestants were said to have been stripped naked 'whereof about a hundred murther'd within a church'. Other stories said that in Fermanagh 'a child of Thomas Stratton boiled to death in a cauldron', in Tyrone 'a young fat Scotchman murther'd and candles made of his grease'; a story from Tyrone had 'another Scotchman's belly ripped up and the ends of his small guts tied to a tree, then he drawn about till his guts were pulled out that they might try . . . whether a dog's or a Scotchman's guts were longest.'

The stories of atrocities committed on the Protestants were matched by stories of atrocities inflicted on the Catholics.

William of Orange Arrives in England

When William of Orange landed at Torbay in the south of England, the Lord Deputy in Dublin, Richard Talbot, Earl of Tyrconnell, immediately dispatched three Irish regiments to England to help James II and he also set about securing Ireland for him. He raised a large, irregular, untrained and undisciplined army of Catholics and took possession of the most important places throughout the country. He also ordered Colonel Mountjoy and Lieutenant Colonel Robert Lundy, the officers commanding the regiment based in Derry, which was then a completely walled city situated on the Donegal side of the River Foyle, to march south to Dublin on 20 November, 1688, to replace the regiments sent to England.

At the same time, Lord MacDonnell, third Earl of Antrim, was ordered to raise a regiment of Catholic Irish and Scots to march to Derry to garrison that city. Lord MacDonnell, at the age of seventy-six, was quite willing to obey but he took his time. He wanted only fine physical specimens over six feet tall in his army, so recruitment went slowly. Consequently the regiment was not ready to take over Derry on 20 November. Colonel Mountjoy could not wait, so he marched his regiment out of the city three days later, leaving it without a garrison.

James II, the first English king to attend the opening of an Irish parliament, wore a crown specially made for him in Dublin.

By December 1688 Antrim had organised his regiment of 1,200 'Redshanks', as the bare-legged Highlanders were called, and got ready to march to Derry.

The 'Comber Letter'

In the same week as Antrim's Redshanks were marching to Derry the notorious 'Comber letter' was found in the street of the village of Comber in County Down. It was addressed to the local Protestant leader, Lord Mount-Alexander, and dated 3 December, 1688. It was written in a semiliterate hand and unsigned. The letter read:

To my Lord this deliver with haste and care.

Good my Lord, I have written to you to let you know that all our Irishmen through Ireland is sworn that on the ninth day of this month they are to fall on to kill and murder man, wife and child; and I desire your Lordship to take care of yourself and all others that are judged by our men to be heads, for whosoever can kill any of you, they are to have a captain's place; so my desire to your honour is to look to yourself and give other noblemen warning, and go not out either night or day without a good guard with you, and let no Irishman come near you, whatsoever he be; so this is all from him who was your father's friend, and is your friend, and will be, though I dare not be known as yet for fear of my life.

The writer's identity has never been established and controversy has persisted to the present day as to whether it was genuine or a hoax. A strong pointer to the fact that the letter was indeed a hoax was the discovery of several similar letters throughout Ulster.

Local Protestants immediately assumed the Comber letter was genuine and copies of the letter soon circulated throughout the province and even further. Among those who received the letter were Alderman Tomkins in Derry and George Phillips in Limavady.

King William of Orange arrived in Carrickfergus in June 1690.

The Redshanks Arrive at Derry

When Antrim's Redshanks passed through Limavady messengers were immediately sent from the town to the inhabitants of Derry to warn them of the Redshanks' approach. The messengers arrived in Derry to find Alderman Tomkins reading his copy of the Comber letter to a group of worried townsfolk.

The Protestants of Derry had a difficult choice: should they admit Antrim's Redshanks and be slaughtered or should they refuse entry to them and so commit an act of rebellion against the Lord Deputy Tyrconnell, who was acting on behalf of the lawful King James?

The news that the Redshanks were rapidly approaching the east bank of the Foyle, opposite the walled town which was then totally on the west bank, added great urgency to the necessity to come to a decision. While the arguments for and against opening the gates went on, the first of the enemy had started crossing the river in boats. Two of their officers landed on the west shore and marched to the walls on 18 December, 1688 where they presented their warrant, which demanded quarters for their men and forage for their horses.

The Apprentice Boys Shut the Gates

A fault in the warrant (it had not been signed) allowed the sheriffs to delay, and at this point thirteen apprentice boys ran to the main guard house and seized the keys. They then rushed to Ferryquay Gate where they raised the drawbridge and shut the gate in the faces of the astonished Redshank officers.

The Redshanks stood around, expecting that the gate would be opened again but one of the citizens, James Morrison, shouted to them to be off. While they waited he called to an invisible colleague to 'bring the great gun here'

When copies of the Comber letter were circulated in Dublin Lord Deputy Tyrconnell summoned leading Protestant businessmen to Dublin Castle and called for the wrath of God upon his head if the report was not 'a cursed, a blasted, a confounded lie.' When they obviously did not believe him he hurled his wig on the fire and threw his hat after it!

The thirteen apprentice boys in Derry were Henry Campsie, William Crookshank, Alexander Irwin, William Cairns, Samuel Hunt, James Spike, John Cunningham, James Steward, Samuel Harvey, Robert Morrison, Alexander Cunningham, Robert Sherrard and Daniel Sherrard.

Derry's walls were constructed between 1613 and 1618 and had an outer stone section two metres thick. The earth in front of the walls was dug out to form a ditch about three metres deep and nine metres wide. This ditch ran along the whole length of the wall except for the part overlooking the Bogside on the northern side (where the ground was very steep) and at the part of the wall along the river where the Guildhall is at present. The earth removed was used to form an earthen rampart three and a half metres thick behind the wall. Derry was the last walled city to be built in western Europe and is the only town in Ireland where the complete surrounding stone wall survives.

The Irish soldiers at Derry were very badly equipped. One regiment had only seven muskets for 600 men and those that had them barely knew how to use them. The main type of musket was the matchlock in which the gunpowder had to be ignited by a glowing piece of tow (called match). Wind and rain played havoc with its effectiveness.

and at this the Redshanks took to their heels. Some shots had indeed been fired from the walls and they had fled in panic, not knowing that the shots were blanks.

Meanwhile the Earl of Antrim and George Phillips of Limavady were in a coach following in the wake of their troops but as they got within a short distance of Derry they saw groups of men running away from the city. They were members of the Redshanks, many of them having got rid of their boots so they could run faster. Lord Antrim decided to send Phillips to the city to find out how the situation was. The gate was opened to Phillips and he then arranged to be 'publicly threatened with confinement' if he did not support the citizens. He reported back to Antrim that he was being detained against his will and that he would strongly advise him not to try to force an entry to the city. Antrim, being a sensible man, decided to withdraw his troops to Coleraine and Phillips then cheerfully agreed to accept the governorship of Derry! (He had previously been governor under Charles II whom James had succeeded in 1685.)

Although the gates had been closed, the city was not prepared to withstand an attack. There was a great shortage of arms and less than five hundred men capable of using them.

Support for the city defenders then began to arrive from the surrounding countryside and soon six companies of soldiers were formed for the defence, totalling about 7,000 men. These were organised by David Cairns, a Derry lawyer and uncle of one of the apprentice boys, who had ridden in from his house in Tyrone. He then sailed off to London with a letter seeking arms and ammunition from the Irish Society (the company set up in London to manage the Plantation of Ulster).

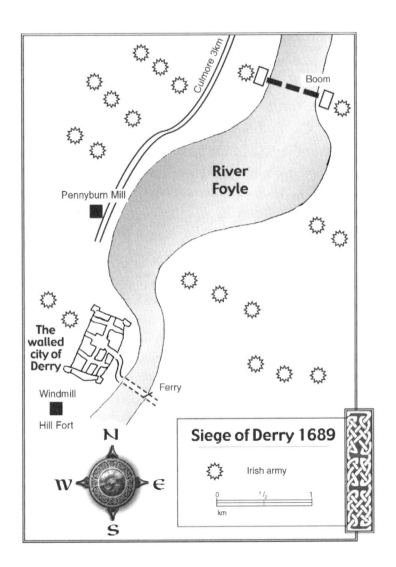

Tyrconnell Sends in the Army

Lord Deputy Tyrconnell heard of Derry's defiance and, having as usual stamped on his wig and thrown it on the fire, immediately sent the army under Colonels Mountjoy and Lundy back to Derry to retake the city. The army reached the city just before Christmas but Mountjoy's request for admittance to the defenders was rejected with the statement that under no circumstances would they allow any Catholic into the city. Eventually they agreed that if all of Antrim's Redshanks withdrew they would allow two totally Protestant companies, under the command of Lieutenant Colonel Robert Lundy, to enter. Lundy was then appointed city governor by the citizens and Mountjoy returned to Dublin.

Lundy was in a delicate position – he was an officer in Tyrconnell's army which was loyal to King James but he was a Protestant in a Protestant city loyal to William.

Help Arrives from England

David Cairns had reached London by now and was granted an interview with William who agreed to send the ship *Deliverance* to Derry with badly needed supplies of 8,000 muskets, 450 barrels of gunpowder and £8,595 in cash. The ship's captain, William Hamilton, was also given a new commission appointing Lundy as governor but this was not to be handed over until Lundy had taken a new oath of allegiance to King William. When the *Deliverance* arrived in Derry on 22 March Lundy took the oath in private on the ship but he later refused to take it in public. He did, however, attend a public ceremony in Derry in March to celebrate the coronation of William and Mary. (Controversy has persisted about whether Lundy ever did swear allegiance, but since the ship's captain, Hamilton, was intensely loyal to William it is very likely that Lundy did indeed take the oath.)

When the Jacobite force first arrived on the eastern side of the River Foyle opposite the walled city they fired a single cannon shot across the river, which struck the city wall beside Ferryquay Gate. The citizens of Derry were angry that no shot was fired in reply but the simple reason for this was that the gunners had no ammunition to fire back at them. A report later said that 'when the enemy appeared near the town the Gunner had no ammunition to fire at them, as the Gunner himself then told them.'

The weekly ration for a soldier was fixed at 'a salmon and a half, two pounds of salt beef and four quarts of oatmeal'.

Mortars were frequently used in sieges at the time. These could fire shells for quite long distances and at the siege of Derry mortars fired shells into the city from a position hundreds of metres away across the Foyle. The shells were filled with powder and had a fuse. The shells were placed in the gun barrel with the fuse sticking out towards the front and this was ignited by a gunner inserting a long piece of burning match down the barrel. This was an extremely hazardous manoeuvre, as can easily be imagined.

The gunners had to estimate the length of time the piece of fuse took to burn down to the charge; if it was too short there was great danger that the shell would explode in the barrel, with the obvious tragic consequences. A favourite method of estimating the proper length of fuse was to test it by seeing what length would burn during the recital of the Apostles' Creed.

Another method of lighting the fuse was by having the shells put in the barrel with the fuse towards the charge and hoping that the blast would light the fuse.

When Cairns returned from London on 10 April with further assurances from the new king the city council held a meeting at which they passed a resolution pledging their loyalty to William and Mary, and Lundy was one of the signatories.

Because the situation in Derry was becoming increasingly desperate many of the inhabitants started to leave the city. (Lundy was later accused of encouraging this exodus.) The more resolute citizenry decided to erect a pair of gallows on the southwest corner of the city's wall as a warning of the fate awaiting deserters.

King James Plucks Up Courage

When James heard of all that Tyrconnell was doing on his behalf he mustered up the courage to come to Ireland and landed in Kinsale in Cork on 12 March, 1689, the first English king to come to Ireland since Richard II in 1399. He was accompanied by a small number of French officers and some Irish troops, among whom was one officer called Patrick Sarsfield, who was six feet tall, well built and thirty-eight years old. The overall commander of the forces was a French general named Rosen.

Just one day after his arrival in Dublin, James summoned a parliament in the city to meet on 7 May, 1689. James himself attended the opening ceremony, wearing his robes and a crown specially made for him in Dublin. Never before had an English king attended the opening of an Irish parliament.

Meanwhile the attempts to capture Derry were getting no further but when James was told that he only had to appear at the gates of that city and they would be thrown open to him, he set out for the North. His journey was very miserable, as the country was completely desolate, but he eventually joined his commander, James Hamilton, and his army a few

The tactic for capturing a walled city current at the time was to concentrate the fire of about six cannon at one chosen spot. Although there was a contingent of experienced French artillery men among the Jacobites at Derry they didn't seem to know the rules and 'their cannon produced no effect worth notice. They discharged not at all at the wall but over it, among houses and at the sallying parties.' The defenders discovered that the cannonballs fired into the city could fit their own guns and soon the cannonballs raining on the city were being returned as quickly as they came in.

The Jacobite leader Rosen was a soldier of fortune from what is present-day Estonia. He joined the French army as a private and eventually reached the rank of colonel-general. It was said of him that his temper was savage, his manners were coarse and his language was a strange jargon compounded of various dialects of French and German.

It is claimed that Lieutenant-Colonel Robert Lundy, Governor of Derry, arrived at Cladyford as the Protestant defence was beginning to crumble and is reported to have sworn a great oath and saying, 'Gentlemen, I see you will not fight' and fled, shouting as he went, 'You are all lost, shift for yourselves.'

kilometres south of Derry. Hamilton had about 7,000 soldiers at his command and together with another force under the French general, Rosen, they set up camp at a crossing on the River Foyle, twenty-four kilometres south of the city near Lifford and Clady.

Lundy under Suspicion

Meanwhile the citizens of Derry were beginning to have doubts about the competence of their new governor, Colonel Lundy. He began to pull back outlying garrisons to the city and the notion began to grow among the citizens that he was in favour of not defending the city. He did, however, post cavalry and dragoons opposite likely crossing points for the Jacobite army.

Rosen's first attempt to cross the Foyle at the ford at Clady, three miles upstream from Lifford, was successfully repulsed by the Protestant cavalry under Captain Crofton and Major Hamill. Even so, it became clear that ammunition was extremely scarce among the defenders, with only three rounds apiece and hardly any powder. By April 15 more troops from Derry arrived to defend the river but the Jacobites still attempted another crossing near a partially destroyed bridge. The odds against them were of the order of ten to one but in spite of these odds the Jacobite cavalry plunged into the river, each trooper towing an infantry man who clung to his horse's tail. The Protestant defenders under Lundy fired briskly at the crossing troops but to no effect. The Jacobite troops managed to struggle to the opposite bank but they were in a very vulnerable position as they had hardly a single dry shot among them. The Protestants were no better off, however, as they had scarcely any ammunition, wet or dry. Their fears greatly increased as they saw the Jacobite infantry begin to repair the bridge and soon the defenders took to their heels with terrified cries of 'To Derry! To Derry!'.

The Irish cavalry rode off in pursuit and overtook and killed about four hundred of the infantry, although the fleeing cavalry were beyond them. (These same men who fled from Cladyford were the same who resolutely withstood the prolonged siege behind Derry's walls for the next three months.) No sooner had Lundy reached the safety of the city walls than he ordered that the gates be closed and in doing so excluded thousands of his own men, variously reckoned to be anything from 4,000 to 8,000 men. Among them was the Reverend Walker, a military clergyman of great ability and courage, who managed to force his way into the city the next morning. The gates were again closed and only reopened when an army captain threatened to blow a sentry's head off if he didn't open the gate to a crowd outside.

A Relief Fleet Arrives in Lough Foyle

It was while the Protestants were suffering defeat at Cladyford that a relief fleet under Colonel John Cunningham arrived in Lough Foyle on April 15. The next morning Cunningham and several officers made their way ashore to Lundy's house where they met many of the local gentry and garrison officers. George Walker tried to gain entry but was forcibly ejected. Cunningham handed over a letter from King William urging Lundy to defend the city and promising that further reinforcements would soon be sent.

Lundy had already decided to surrender, however, and the group agreed that the troops should return to England. To protect themselves from any possible repercussions Lundy proposed that everyone present should take an oath of secrecy about what had taken place. Although an oath of secrecy was rejected they did agree to something similar, namely, 'upon their honour not to discover what resolution they had taken'. They were also to pretend that Cunningham's return to his fleet was simply to bring his troops to the city.

The meeting's deception was all in vain, however, as they had forgotten the one silent witness to the whole sordid affair – the note-taking secretary. Very soon their perfidy was known to the population of the city.

At this critical point a new leader emerged – a young Ulster Scot named Adam Murray, who worked on his father's farm at Ling in the valley of the Faughan just southeast of Derry. He had command of a body of cavalry at Cladyford and when he heard of the council's intention to surrender he immediately set out for the town. When he arrived he found Shipquay Gate closed and, when he demanded that the gate be opened to him, George Walker was sent to reason with him. Walker's suggestion that he could be hauled up and over the walls on a rope was angrily dismissed by Murray who said he would ride in at the head of his men or not at all. The captain of the guard ended the impasse by throwing open the gate so Murray and his men could enter Derry.

Murray Organises the Defences

Murray soon found that most of the citizens and soldiers were totally against surrender. He encouraged them to stand firm and told them that more help would come from England and that the first thing they should do was to 'expel the traitor and his false cabal'. He asked all who agreed with him to wear a white badge on their left arms, and soon thousands were doing so. They marched through the city, cursing Lundy and his cowardly allies and shouting their determination to

During his escape from Derry, Lundy disguised himself as a private soldier and is said to have escaped over the east wall by climbing a pear tree growing against it. He was carrying 'a load of match' on his back to aid his disguise. Match was the slow-burning cord that was used to fire the matchlock musket at the time, but later writers mistakenly took it to be matchwood. This is why Lundy's effigy is commonly burned with a bundle of sticks on its back at the annual ceremony commemorating the siege.

Lundy, after he escaped, made his way to Culmore and then to Scotland where he was arrested. He was sent to the Tower of London and tried for treason but was later released on bail and allowed to join the English army. He helped to defend Gibraltar in 1707 in the War of the Spanish Succession. Taken prisoner by the Spanish he was later released in exchange for twenty Spanish soldiers and returned to England. He died in 1717.

The fighting strength of the garrison in Derry varied from about 7,000 at the start of the siege to 4,892 on 25 July to 4,456 on 27 July.

defend the city. The citizens were so angered by Lundy's behaviour that he had to stay in his room with a guard of his own soldiers outside the door to protect him.

The garrison consisted of 7,000 fighting men and 340 officers – eight regiments altogether. Two guns were planted on the flat roof of the cathedral and every gate had a gun commanding the approach.

George Walker and Major Henry Baker (a professional soldier from County Louth) were then chosen to take charge of the defence of the town and surprisingly enough the first thing they did was to invite Lundy to become governor again but he refused. Walker and Baker then became 'the government of the garrison' and they now allowed Lundy to leave the city as he was in danger of being lynched if he remained. He disguised himself and left the city.

With the departure of Lundy the new governors set about organising the city's defences. The city was divided into eight sectors and each sector had a 'home-guard' regiment to defend it. A curfew was introduced and all the town's ammunition was divided into four parts and lodged in four different places.

By this time James and his army were nearing Derry and when he approached Bishop's Gate he stopped about 200 metres from it. Immediately a terrific barrage of cannon and musket fire was directed at them from the walls and the famous cry 'No Surrender' rang out for the first time.

An officer at the king's side was killed and the rest of the soldiers took to their heels, although many were killed. James himself retired out of shooting range and sat on his horse all day watching the city in the pouring rain.

Even at that stage there was the possibility that the city would surrender, for Walker and Baker sent an abject apology to James, saying that a rabble had seized the cannon and fired on the king's army. The king accepted the apology and sent a messenger, 'a lord with a trumpet', to ask for twenty men to be sent to the king to arrange the surrender. Again the city council gave in and appointed the twenty representatives that would leave the city to discuss terms but when they approached the city gates the men on guard threatened them that any man who left would be treated as a traitor. Mindful of the fact that one of the city's officers had previously been shot for trying to escape, the representatives decided to stay put. From that point on, all thought of surrender ceased.

A message was sent to James to the effect that the city was determined to hold out for King William and, realising that no further purpose would be served by remaining at Derry, James, accompanied by Rosen, returned to Dublin.

The Siege Begins

The commander of the Jacobite army at Derry now was the French general, Maumont. His army settled in on the hills surrounding the city, stretching from the south right round to Culmore Fort, which was six kilometres north of the city on Lough Foyle. The fort itself had been in the hands of a Protestant garrison but they surrendered without a fight.

The Jacobite soldiers were very poorly equipped for a long siege. One French officer said that 'most of the soldiers in front of Derry have still only pointed sticks, without iron tips'. When King James had previously inspected one regiment he found that only one gun in a hundred could be fired.

A number of cannon were then put in place on the east bank of the river, particularly opposite the Shipquay Gate, and they commenced shelling the city.

Two days earlier the Protestants had a victory at

Pennyburn, just north of the city. The small village was in their hands and as the Jacobite army moved in to occupy it they were ambushed by some Protestants who lay behind the hedges. This group was later strengthened by a further 500 musketeers from Derry. Hamilton, the leader of the Jacobites, immediately sent for reinforcements and when the commander-in-chief, Maumont, rode to his aid at the head of a small cavalry troop, Maumont himself was killed. The Protestants were driven back to Derry, however, but the Jacobite cavalry riding in pursuit were almost wiped out by the musketeers lying in ambush.

The siege continued, with the Jacobites bombarding the city and small bands of defenders rushing out to repel any Irish who approached the walls. By the end of six weeks up to 3,000 of the besiegers had died of disease or been killed.

At the end of May the Jacobites decided to build a floating boom across the river mouth to prevent relief of the city from the sea and by 4 June it was completed. The boom was made of oak planks at first but when that sank they replaced it with one made of pine. It was bound with chains and cables and attached to each side of the river but the whole assembly could float up and down with the tide.

In the meantime the Jacobites made several determined efforts to attack the city outposts but were beaten back each time. The Derry womenfolk took an active part in the proceedings 'carrying ammunition, match, bread and drink to our men . . . and beating off with stones the grenadiers who came next to our lines'.

A Second Relief Fleet Arrives in Lough Foyle

On 31 May a fleet of thirty ships under the command of Major General Percy Kirke, carrying 5,000 soldiers and a

During the siege of Derry great efforts were made by Major General Kirke to establish communications between the fleet and the city's defenders. He called for volunteers to attempt to make contact with the defenders. Two men – a Scot, James Cromie, and an Irishman, James Roche, stepped forward. Cromie couldn't swim but Roche was a powerful swimmer. A small boat landed the two brave volunteers at Faughan on the eastern bank of the Foyle about eight kilometres from the city. The two men managed to make their way through Irish lines for about three kilometres and then Roche stripped off at a deserted fish house and entered the river to swim the remaining distance. He staggered ashore, nearly dead from cold and exhaustion. When he recovered enough to be aware of his circumstances he found he was in the hands of the city's citizens and that they were about to hang him as a spy.

He managed to convince them that he was a genuine messenger from Kirke by predicting accurately what Kirke's reply would be to a signal from the cathedral steeple. After that he was warmly welcomed by the garrison and he gave them a letter from Kirke and details about the relieving fleet. He told them that there were great supplies on board the ships for them but also gave them the sobering message from Kirke that they should carefully ration their food as their deliverance would take some time.

Roche then set about the arduous return trip with the message that there was only enough food left in the city for four more days. He swam all the way back to the fish house to retrieve his clothes at midnight only to find that Jacobite dragoons were in hiding waiting for him. He managed to evade them and fled totally naked through the woods for five kilometres with the dragoons in hot pursuit. Just as they closed in on him and broke his jaw and a collarbone with a blow from a musket he jumped from a nine-metre cliff into the Foyle. Even then he was not safe, for they fired hundreds of shots and wounded him in the chest, hand and shoulder.

Miraculously he managed to swim back to Derry city where he lay unconscious for an hour. He later made a full recovery from his wounds and was rewarded with a captain's commission in the army of King William and later some lands in County Waterford.

cargo of food, set sail from Liverpool to raise the siege of Derry. On 7 June the delighted Derry garrison saw the masts of three shallow draught ships, the *Greyhound*, the *Fisher* and the *Edward* entering Lough Foyle. After some brisk exchange of fire with the Jacobite land guns the three ships were extremely lucky to escape back to safer waters. Four days later, on 11 June, Kirke's full fleet sailed into view to the intense joy of the garrison who fired off celebratory cannon and rang the cathedral bells. And then, to the rage of the besieged and the puzzlement of the besiegers, Kirke proceeded to do absolutely nothing for six weeks!

There were no means of communication between city and fleet and all efforts at signalling failed. When a large banner was waved four times from the steeple of the cathedral to show that the people were in desperate straits the fleet took it to mean that they were proudly showing off captured enemy colours! Various valiant attempts to send messages by hand between the fleet and city all failed and another six weeks of ever-increasing starvation was to be endured by the desperate inhabitants before they got any relief.

General Rosen Takes Over

In the middle of all this trouble the city got more bad news – the ruthless French General Rosen returned from Dublin on 17 June to take command of the besieging army again. He very soon lived up to his reputation for cruelty by sending word to the city that unless they surrendered he would round up every Protestant he could find and send them into the city. His purpose was to further increase the appalling starvation the citizens were suffering. Not receiving an immediate response to his ultimatum he drove over a thousand Protestant men, women and children to the city's walls in the hope that the

The Scotsman Cromie, the second volunteer to attempt to reach the city had his own story to tell. After Roche set out to swim to Derry he remained in hiding in the woods but was captured by Jacobite soldiers. He was brought to the French officer in command, the Chevalier de Vaundry, who questioned him closely and frightened him sufficiently to bring a false message supposedly from Kirke to the Derry garrison. The Jacobites then invited the city to send out a deputation to parley. This they did and Cromie told them that there was no hope of relief from Kirke. When they asked Cromie why his story was so different from Roche's he pointed out that he was a prisoner of the Jacobites. This hint confirmed their belief that Roche was the genuine messenger.

It had been prearranged that the boat which had landed Roche and Cromie should return to pick them up on 26 June. When it arrived at Faughan, however, the Jacobites, informed by Cromie, were waiting for them. They called on the crew to come ashore but when asked for the password the Jacobites didn't know it. The small boat immediately pulled away and in spite of heavy fire managed to get back to the fleet. It was assumed then that both Cromie and Roche had been captured.

On that same night of 26 June another brave man called McGimpsey volunteered to swim from the city to the fleet. He entered the river at Ship Quay with messages for Kirke in a pig's bladder which was tied to his neck. He never reached the fleet, however, but drowned in the river. His body was later pulled out of the water by the Jacobites who found the letters. These greatly encouraged the besieging army, for the letters stated that 'if you do not send relief we must surrender the garrison in six or seven days'. (In fact the siege was to last another six weeks.)

garrison would be forced to admit them. But the brave refugees called on their friends inside the walls not to give in, telling them that if they surrendered they would all be killed.

The garrison then neatly met threat with counter-threat. They erected a large gallows in full view of the enemy and announced that unless the Protestants in front of the walls were allowed to depart they would hang every Jacobite prisoner they had.

Shortly afterwards the attackers relented, gave the Protestant refugees food and money and allowed them to return to their homes. In response the garrison dismantled the gallows. Later when King James heard what Rosen had done he was furious and said that 'only a barbarous Muscovite' could have thought up such a scheme.

In letters to King James at this time Rosen complained that the reinforcements from Dublin were useless – one regiment had only seven muskets among them, the rest had only sticks! Hamilton's soldiers at Derry were even worse off – more than two thirds of them had 'no swords, belts or bandoliers' and they were dying faster from disease than from battle. One regiment given the task of guarding the chest that contained the money to pay the troops had not been issued with a single round of ammunition! Two or three weeks later Rosen left for France to the great satisfaction of both Jacobites and Williamites.

On 10 July Hamilton again called on the city to surrender by firing a hollow cannonball containing the surrender terms into the grounds of the cathedral. (That cannonball is still on show in St Columb's Cathedral in the city today.) The temptation was great to accept, as the population was on the point of starvation. Even more disheartening was the disappearance of most of the fleet from Lough Foyle on 12 July. On 13 July a deputation was sent to the besieging army

George Walker said that the army besieging Derry lobbed mortar bombs weighing 270 lbs each into the city. These 'contained several pounds of powder in the shell; they plowed up our streets and broke down our houses, so there was no passing the streets or staying within doors.'

During the siege the defenders came on a store of starch from which they made pancakes of starch and tallow. These were not only good food but were found to help cure diarrhoea which was extremely common due to the poor diet of the citizens! George Walker commented that they were 'an infallible cure of the looseness'.

During the hungry days of the siege of Derry 'a certain fat gentleman conceived himself in great danger and, fancying several of the garrison looked at him with a greedy eye, thought fit to hide himself for three days.'

carrying a list of terms which would allow an honourable surrender. Deadlock followed and the delegation was allowed to go back to the city to get the council to agree to surrender by 15 July instead of the proposed 26 July. Hamilton was convinced the council was playing for time in the hope that Kirke would relieve the siege before then.

The council would not agree to yield on the earlier date and then they found out that Kirke had only withdrawn most of his fleet in an attempt to cut off the Jacobites' supply of food from Inch Island in Lough Swilly and also to give the soldiers a break from aboard ship. Messages now passed back and forth between the city and Kirke by the ingenious use of small boys. (Some of them carried messages concealed in their rectums.)

The Plight of the Citizens is Desperate

On 26 July at 3 a.m. 200 men left by Bishop's Gate and another 200 by Butcher's Gate with the intention of capturing some of the Jacobites' cattle. The plan was a failure and the plight of the city's inhabitants was so desperate that men could hardly stand or walk, never mind fight. The besieging army was almost in as bad a state and knew that they had no hope of storming the city; their only hope was to starve it into surrender.

Meanwhile, King William's Marshal Schomberg had written to Kirke to tell him he must try to relieve the city. Kirke selected three small ships, the fifty-ton *Phoenix*, the *Jerusalem* of about the same size, and the 150-ton *Mountjoy* to attempt to break the boom. The warship, the *Dartmouth*, commanded by Captain Leake, was sent as escort.

The plan was that the *Mountjoy* and *Phoenix* would attempt to break the boom, while the *Dartmouth* would engage the enemy guns on each side of the river. The

It was estimated that during the Derry siege 15,000 men, women and children died, many from hunger but most from the fever that raged through the city. 'People died so fast at length as scarce could be found room to inter them, even backsides and gardens were filled with graves, and some thrown in cellars; some whole families were entirely extinct.'

The largest gun on Derry's walls was 'Roaring Meg', so-called because of the tremendous sound it made. It was a gift from the Fishmongers of London in 1642. It is 3.3 metres long and 1.4 metres wide at its thickest part. It still stands silently on guard facing the Derry Guildhall today.

A Captain Holmes said that during the Derry siege 'one bomb slew seventeen persons. I was in the next room one night at my supper and seven men were thrown out of the third room next to that we were in, all killed and some in pieces.'

During the siege of Derry prices of various foods were posted up, giving the price of a dog's head at two shillings and sixpence, a cat at one shilling and sixpence, a rat for one shilling, and horseflesh at one shilling and eightpence a pound.

Marshal Schomberg issued an order to his troops at Derry forbidding 'the Horrid and Detestable Crimes of Prophane Cursing, Swearing and taking God's Holy Name in vain'.

Jerusalem was to be kept in reserve and only to sail when the boom was broken. A longboat crewed by nine seamen from the *Swallow*, which was too big to navigate the river, was to help in the task of breaking the boom.

Attempts to Break Through the Blockade

At 7 o'clock on the calm Sunday evening of 28 July the *Dartmouth* led the way, followed by the three smaller ships and the longboat. While the *Dartmouth* exchanged gunfire with the Jacobite guns at Culmore, the two small ships slipped by and made for the boom. By now the air was so calm that their sails were useless and the ships had to rely on the incoming tide to carry them onwards. The heavier *Mountjoy*, commanded by a Captain Brown, sailed into the boom and broke part of it. The sailors in the longboat then used axes to make a gap in the boom.

The *Mountjoy* meanwhile had rebounded from the boom and got stuck fast in the mud. Two regiments of Jacobite cavalry immediately rode into the shallow water to capture the boat whose crew prepared to resist all attempts at boarding. The *Mountjoy* fired off three of her cannon at the approaching cavalry and not only did this cause considerable damage but fortuitously enough, the recoil drove the ship back out into the deeper water. Then, towed by the longboat, she followed the *Phoenix* through the gap that had been made right up to the city. The joyful citizens rushed to the Ship Quay and started unloading their precious cargo.

In the midst of all this the brave Captain Brown lay dead upon the deck of his ship, the *Mountjoy*. He had been shot in the head when the ship had been stuck in the mudbank. (He was later buried in Derry Cathedral.)

Three days after the boom was breached and 105 days from the start of the siege the Jacobite army withdrew.

Captain Brown of the leading ship running the blockade of Derry, the *Mountjoy*, was a Derryman. His wife and children were in the beleaguered city and he was determined to do all in his power to get through. He sailed his ship straight at the boom. The barrier was severely damaged but the ship rebounded into the shallows of the Foyle and went aground. The helpless *Mountjoy* lay on her side and soon came under attack from the land guns of the besiegers. All seemed lost until the captain ordered that all the ship's cannon be fired simultaneously on the landward side. This was done and the subsequent recoil of the guns propelled the ship once more into deeper waters.

Because its walls have never been breached Derry earned the name the 'Maiden City'.

The BATTLE of the BOYNE
(1690)

King James Arrives in Ireland

When King James was displaced from the English throne he had first fled to France. Then in March 1689 he travelled to Ireland in the hope that he could recover his position. He regarded Ireland as a stepping stone to realising his ambition, whereas the Irish had more interest in reversing the Cromwellian settlement which had given Irish land to soldiers and adventurers than any desire to restore the Stuarts to the throne.

King William was aware of the threat posed by James in Ireland and after the siege of Derry he was able to devote more time to Irish affairs. He sent Frederick Herman, Duke of Schomberg to Ireland on 13 August, 1689, with an army of 14,500 men. The seventy-three-year-old German Protestant landed in Bangor Bay at the head of an army composed mostly of Dutch Huguenots. Later reinforcements boosted

Although the battle of the Boyne took place on 1 July, 1690, it is now traditionally celebrated by Northern Orangemen on 12 July each year. This is due to the revision of the Julian calendar in March 1582 by the order of Pope Gregory XIII. To make the calendar more accurate eleven days were added to all previous dates.

The mounted men in the battle of the Boyne included types new to Irish warfare – dragoons. These were simply infantry who were given horses to make them more mobile. In battle they dismounted and fought on foot. Another type was the mounted grenadier whose weapon was a small, hollow cast-iron ball filled with gunpowder. A piece of slow-burning match protruded from the ball and when this was lit the grenadier would throw the ball. The 'grenade' would then explode. Grenadiers carried three grenades, each of which weighed 1.4 kilograms.

Marshal Schomberg's army consisted of four cavalry regiments, one dragoon regiment and eighteen infantry regiments, most of whom had never been in battle before.

The name 'dragoon' comes from a type of short musket called the 'dragon'. Because early dragoons were no match for true cavalry they were gradually trained to be more expert horsemen and so the term 'dragoon' came to mean medium cavalry.

The flintlock musket of the period fired a single lead ball each time. The ball and the charge were contained in a small paper cartridge. The soldier would firmly hold the ball through the paper, bite off one end of the cartridge, and pour the powder down the barrel. He would then drop the ball down after it and ram the cartridge paper down with the 'ramrod' attached to the barrel.

his army to over 20,000 men. Schomberg had an international reputation but did little to enhance it in his Irish campaign. First he led his army south to Dundalk but then returned to Lisburn, County Antrim, and settled down there to over-winter in a fortified camp. The heavy rains of October came and the lack of proper accommodation, coupled with bad food and inadequate clothing, left the troops in poor condition. The outbreak of dysentery ('the bloody flux') swept away nearly half his army so that he was forced to send for replacements to restart the campaign. By the following May troopships arrived daily, packed with English, Dutch and German soldiers.

King William Arrives in Carrickfergus

On 14 June 1690 William himself landed at Carrickfergus with 15,000 men to take command. He immediately set about reorganising the army, which now totalled about 36,000 men, and intended to march on Dublin by the most direct route. Both William and James considered that Dublin was worth fighting for, as they regarded the possession of the capital to be the key to the whole country.

Lord Deputy Tyrconnell had assembled an army for James of about 20,000 men but, while the calibre of the men was extremely good, they were poorly trained and equipped. Many carried only staves and others had scythes instead of pikes. (Some of James' best soldiers were stationed in various garrisons such as Drogheda and so took no part in the coming battle at the Boyne.)

A force of 6,000 men had arrived from France on 12 March, 1690, to assist James but he was disappointed to find that only three of the six battalions were French and the rest were composed of Walloons and, mostly Protestant,

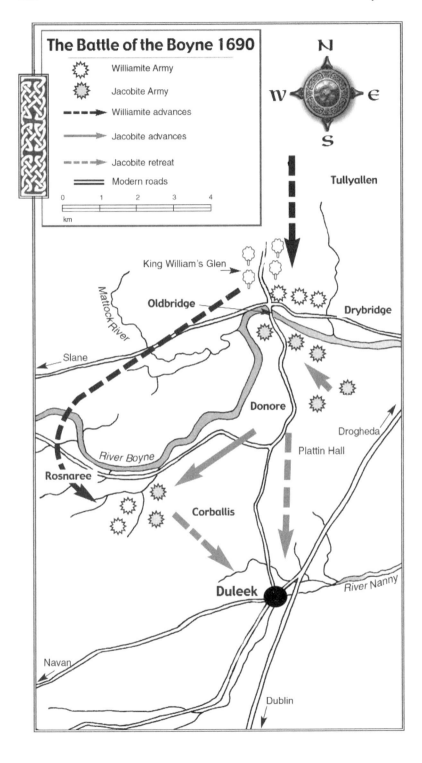

The Battle of the Boyne 1690

Germans. The force was under the command of a diminutive fifty-eight-year-old courtier, Comte Lauzun.

Before the Battle

The Jacobite army, under King James and the Earl of Tyrconnell, took up a position on the south bank of the river not far inland from the then small town of Drogheda. James had his headquarters at Donore and he placed his four cavalry squadrons at Plattin Hall. He positioned his foot soldiers at Oldbridge where he hoped that William's main attack would occur but because this was by no means certain he kept his dragoons as a mobile force to deal with any river crossing elsewhere.

There were several weaknesses in James' position: it was within a loop in the river which allowed the possibility of William outflanking him; the northern bank of the Boyne was higher than the south bank; and the deep ravine, now known as King William's Glen, allowed William's army to approach under cover.

The Jacobite army was not long enough in place to be able to really fortify their positions and this was a worry as the river was fordable in a number of places. A wooden bridge at Slane was also a weak point, so they destroyed the bridge before the Williamite army arrived.

William Has a Narrow Escape

The very next day, June 30, William's army appeared on the northern slopes of the river and the Jacobite artillery started a heavy bombardment of the enemy's positions towards the end of that day. William's first impression of the Boyne was that it would be nearly impossible to ford it in the face of enemy fire.

As William and five of his leading officers began a

When William landed in Carrickfergus his army brought with them more than forty pieces of artillery: six- and twelve-pounder demi-culverins, nineteen- and twenty-four-pounder cannon and mortars. Some of the guns were so big that each one needed sixteen horses to pull it. William had more than 2,000 horses for this purpose.

When William was urged to allow one regiment to make an initial attempt to ford the Boyne he would not allow it as he was determined never to undertake anything on a Monday, which he considered unlucky. In fact, it was on a Monday that he was nearly killed while surveying the Jacobite positions at the Boyne.

A Jacobite account of the incident at King William's Glen tells how 'Six shots were fired at William, one whereof fell and struck off the top of the Duke of Würrtemberg's pistol and the whiskers of his horse, and another tore the King's coat on his shoulder.' The torn coat was retained by William's aide-de-camp, Colonel Wetherall, and later exhibited in England and Ireland. The Jacobite gunners never knew how close they had become to altering the history, not only of Ireland, but of Europe as a whole.

Marshal Schomberg complained at the battle conference in Mellifont Abbey that he was more used to giving orders than receiving them.

The Duke of Würrtemberg, commander of the Danish troops, was carried across the Boyne on the shoulders of his grenadiers – the tallest of his men. He later reported that some Irish infantry in his army behaved badly in the battle (and in fact one battalion refused to obey an order to advance and turned and fled from the battlefield).

reconnaissance of the scene they rode to what is now called King William's Glen, dismounted and proceeded to have a picnic! The king was recognised by some Jacobite officers who could not believe their luck and had two field guns quietly brought into position behind a hedge. A Williamite account records:

> They did not offer to fire till his majesty was mounted and then he and the rest, riding softly the same way back, their gunner fired a piece which killed us two horses and a man, about a hundred yards above where the king was but immediately came a second which had almost been a fatal one, for it grazed upon the bank of the river, and in the rising slanted upon the king's right shoulder took out a piece of his coat and tore the skin and flesh and afterwards broke the head of a gentleman's pistol.
>
> Mister Coningsby, seeing his majesty struck, rid up and put his handkerchief upon the place. His majesty took little notice of it but rid on for about forty yards further where there was a high bank on either side but it being open below we returned the very same way again, the enemy's cannon firing on us all the while. They did some damage among our horse, killing two of the guards and about nine of Colonel Coy's horses, with three troopers and also some more out of Colonel Byerley's and other regiments.

William was rushed off to get his wound dressed but the rumour spread that he had been killed. Afterwards William called for a cloak to cover the hole in his jacket and rode around the ranks of his men to reassure them that he was uninjured. (In fact the news of his 'death' reached Paris, where there were bonfires lit in premature celebrations.)

William wore his Star and Garter during the battle of the Boyne but so confused was the battle that he was almost shot by one of his own Enniskillen soldiers who aimed a cocked musket at him till he called out, 'What, are you angry with your friends?'

William had another close shave at Donore when a musket ball shot off the heel of his boot and another shattered one of his pistols. William remarked at the time, 'It's well it came no nearer.'

One report of the time said that most of the Jacobite horsemen

> that charged so desperately were drunk with brandy, each man that morning having received half a pint as his share, but it seems the foot had not so large a portion or at least they did not deserve it so well.

One Jacobite officer wrote that the soldiers fleeing from the Boyne to Duleek threw away their muskets and shoes. Later the Williamite soldiers kept themselves warm by making bonfires of the pikes and muskets thrown away by the Irish.

It was the English rather than the Irish who were 'wearing of the green' at the Boyne because the Williamite soldiers were ordered to wear a sprig of green leaves to distinguish them from the enemy. The Jacobites in turn were ordered to wear a white cockade in their hats but as these were difficult to get they simply stuck a piece of white paper in them instead.

Tactics Are Planned

The Williamite command, including William, Marshal Schomberg, Count Solms, who was leader of the Dutch, and others, held a battle conference that night at Mellifont Abbey to plan tactics for the coming battle. It was decided that one third of the army led by the marshal's son, Count Meinhard Schomberg, would head for the fords at Rosnaree and Slane as a diversionary tactic to draw off a large part of James' army. As soon as this force had crossed the river the main part of the army would make a full frontal attack at Oldbridge.

When the younger Schomberg got advance warning that the bridge at Slane was down he headed for Rosnaree. It was 8 a.m. on a beautiful sunny morning when he arrived at the ford on the northern side of the river. On the opposite side was one regiment of dragoons and three field guns under the command of Sir Niall O'Neill but this tiny force of 500 men was no match for the enemy's 8,000. O'Neill's men did manage to delay the crossing for half an hour but were then swept aside. Those that were able, galloped from the scene, taking their fatally wounded commander with them. By ten o'clock William knew of Schomberg's success and despatched a supporting force under the Scottish Lieutenant General Douglas to join him.

On the Jacobite side the French were the first to hear of the crossing at Rosnaree and immediately Lauzun jumped to the false conclusion that the main attack was going to be made there. James too agreed to allow Lauzun and his French brigade, six guns and some cavalry to attack Schomberg. Some time later James formed the opinion that the main thrust would come at Rosnaree and ordered that most of the army should follow Lauzun. The mounted brigades under Major General Patrick Sarsfield and the Scots-Jacobite General Thomas Maxwell now proceeded inland along the

The 'Lilliburlero' was a poem said to represent Irish Catholics gloating at the appointment of Tyrconnell as Lord Deputy in January 1687. Its opening line was 'Ho Brother Teague dost hear de decree' and ends 'Now, now de Hereticks all go down . . . By Chreist and St Patrick the Nation's our own.' The chorus of 'Lilli Burlero Bullen-a-la' is said to refer to the lily, symbol of the orange party.

The tune is attributed to the Whig leader, Thomas Wharton, who claimed to have 'whistled a king out of three kingdoms'. It later became a standard with orange bands.

Marshal Schomberg said that his men at the Boyne were so untrained that only one in four could even fire their muskets and 'those that did thought they had done a feat if the gun fired, never minding what they shot at'!

Dutch soldiers of the time carried a kind of wooden *chevaux de frise* which was extremely effective against cavalry. It was a portable fence with sharpened wooden stakes sticking out at all angles to provide a fearsome obstacle. The Dutch troops at the Boyne did not have such a fence with them and the Irish cavalry inflicted heavy losses on them.

The type of cannon used at the period was prepared for firing by inserting a charge of powder down the barrel. This was done by means of a ladle at the end of a stick and it was followed by a wad of rags rammed tightly down on top of the gunpowder. A cannonball was then rolled down the barrel. A hole in the top of the barrel over the powder charge was then filled with priming powder. The gun was fired by igniting the priming powder by means of a glowing cord (match) and the flash of the powder ignited the large charge inside the barrel. A stick pushed into the ground near the guns would hold a long length of burning match from which shorter lengths could be lit and brought to the cannon.

river and as they did so they could see Douglas' army marching in the same direction on the northern bank. The Irish army was now split in two, with the main army facing the enemy at the ford of Rosnaree and Tyrconnell left at Oldbridge with less than 7,500 men. Opposite on the other bank, although out of sight, was half of William's army with the commander-general, Marshal Schomberg, and Count Solms, who was in charge of the attempted crossing. The Irish at Oldbridge were outnumbered by more than two to one.

The Battle Begins

William ordered the attack at 10.30 in the morning. Three battalions of blue-coated Dutch guards moved towards the river at Oldbridge with banners flying, drums beating and to the tune of 'Lilliburlero' playing on the fifes. When they reached the water the men started to wade across eight abreast, with their muskets and powder held high above their heads.

Waiting on the other side were the Irish troops lined up in battalions. They held their fire until the Dutch were halfway across and then they opened up. The volley from the first platoon was followed a few seconds later by the second platoon, which was followed in turn by the third platoon. Then the rest of the company started firing, by which time the whole process could be repeated.

The tremendous amount of smoke generated meant that neither side could see the other but the troops kept blindly firing nevertheless.

As the opposing sides closed, fierce hand-to-hand fighting began but gradually the heavily outnumbered Irish troops gave way. When Tyrconnell, who was then sixty years old and in bad health, noticed this he ordered his cavalry to charge. James Fitzjames, Duke of Berwick and illegitimate son of King James, led the thousand-strong cavalry charge down to

There were different types of cannonballs used: solid ones, hollow ones filled with gunpowder and with a fuse sticking out of them, and hollow 'shells' filled with pieces of metal, stones or musket balls.

During the Williamite war both sides used bundles of brushwood and hurdles to spread on soft boggy ground to allow them to cross. William's army even crossed rivers by building bridges on tin pontoons much like armies do today.

Many of William's soldiers had more modern flintlocks. These could fire sixteen balls for every two kilograms of lead as against twelve for the matchlocks and their rate of fire was double the old ones.

When Marshal Schomberg was killed at the Boyne King William is credited with urging his soldiers to further effort by composing the following poem on the spot!

> Brave boys be not dismayed
> For the loss of our commander
> For God will be our King this day
> And I'll be general under.

The Reverend Walker went to join King William when he landed at Carrickfergus in 1690. He accompanied the Williamite army to Drogheda and there he was killed by a 'stray shot' during the battle of the Boyne. Walker was buried where he died on the banks of the Boyne. Thirteen years later his widow had his body removed and reburied in his little church in Donoughmore in County Tyrone.

In 1938 it was discovered that the casket, supposedly containing his bones, in fact contained thigh bones from two different males. It was suspected that Walker's widow had been swindled and indeed the remains of George Walker may still rest 'on the green grassy slopes of the Boyne'.

Oldbridge. King William was worried by this turn of events and his secretary later wrote,

> The king had a good deal of apprehension for them, there not being any hedge or ditch for them or any horse to support them, and I was so near his majesty as to hear him say softly to himself, 'My poor guards, my poor guards', but when he saw them stand their ground and fire by platoon so that the Irish cavalry were forced to run away in great disorder, he breathed out as people do after holding their breath upon a fright or suspense and said he had seen his guards do that which he had never seen foot do in his life.

Marshal Schomberg and George Walker are Killed

Schomberg rode forward to join the battle but was immediately shot dead. Some commentators claim that he was accidentally shot by his own men but that is extremely unlikely. Other accounts tell of him being twice hacked with sabres and then shot in the neck by a Brian O'Toole who had recognised him. O'Toole himself was then killed after 'fighting like a lion'.

Another notable casualty was the Reverend George Walker of the siege of Derry fame. He was shot in the stomach and died in minutes. He was immediately stripped of his fine clothes by 'Scots-Irish' who also pocketed his belongings. When William was informed of his death he showed little regret, merely asking, 'What brought him here?'

William then decided to cross the river and, led by a local Protestant, made for a ford a mile below Oldbridge. He successfully made the crossing at the head of Enniskillen, Dutch and Danish cavalry but his horse got bogged down on the far side so that he had to dismount. He struggled through the mud 'so as to be near out of breath'. (William was indeed a sufferer from asthma.)

The cavalry proper were armed with swords, pistols and carbines. Their tactic was to charge headlong into the enemy, discharge their single-shot carbines and then lay about them with their swords.

The infantry regiments had a few companies of grenadiers who carried a pouch full of grenades to throw at the enemy. The use of pikes was much less at this time and generally there were six muskets to each pike.

The tactics employed by the musketeers were for the first three ranks to fire in unison, the first rank crouching, the second rank kneeling, and the third rank standing. After firing, the three ranks retired to the rear and new men took their place.

It was at this time that the practice of attaching a bayonet to the musket came into use. At first the bayonet was plugged into the barrel and so the musket could not be fired. Later types were attached to the top of the musket barrel by means of rings. The Williamite soldiers at the Boyne had the earlier type but the Jacobites had none at all.

The Williamite soldiers had uniforms of red coats as had the Jacobites, but many of the latter soldiers had to make do with coats of varying colours such as grey, blue and brownish-grey.

The infantry on both sides had broad-brimmed hats and loosely fitting coats with shirt cuffs extending beyond the coat sleeves.

James Fitzjames, Duke of Berwick and illegitimate son of King James, described Tyrconnell thus:

> A man of very good sense, very obliging, but immoderately vain and full of cunning. He had not a military genius but much courage. From the time of the Boyne he sank prodigiously, being become as irresolute in his mind as in his person.

He led this party to Donore where they engaged in battle with some Irish troops. In the confusion and smoke some Enniskilleners indiscriminately attacked both friend and foe, but at the end of the battle Donore was in William's hands.

The Jacobites Concede Defeat

It was evident now to Tyrconnell that the Boyne was lost. He gave orders to Lieutenant General Hamilton to delay the enemy as long as possible and rode away to organise the retreat to Duleek and beyond.

Drogheda surrendered the day after the Boyne battle, having been granted liberal terms: the garrison could go to Athlone but could not bring their arms; clergy and any citizens who wished could go with them; and there would be no looting in the town. In fact the English regiment that took over Drogheda 'took care to preserve the town from the violence of the soldiers'.

When the rout of the Jacobites had begun, James and Lauzun were in a precarious position as they were being threatened on two sides by William's forces. They decided to also make for Duleek with their cavalry. Lauzun was very concerned for the safety of the king and kept urging his cavalry to go faster and faster. When it was pointed out that the infantry would be left unprotected Lauzun replied that the king's safety was paramount.

From Duleek, James set out for Dublin, escorted by Patrick Sarsfield's regiment of horse and dragoons. He reached the capital on the night of 1 July and went to the house of Lady Tyrconnell. When she asked him what he would like to eat for supper he replied that 'after the "breakfast" he had been given that day he had little stomach for supper'. That night Tyrconnell sent an urgent message to James urging him to go immediately to France. (Lauzun also sent a message to the same effect.)

In June 1689 James desperately needed more money for his military activities in Ireland and he appealed to the Irish Parliament for more funds. It was decided to raise the necessary finance by issuing brass and copper coinage. Coins to the value of over £1,000,000 in sixpences, shillings, half-crowns and crowns were minted from bells, gun-metal and pewter. (Many cannons of the period were made of brass.) The government pledged to redeem the coins at a later date. By the spring of 1690 the value of the 'brass money' had fallen so low that a half-crown was only worth a penny of the old money and fifty shillings could only buy one guinea. The brass money was constantly mocked in anti-Jacobite propaganda, the Protestants claiming that William had saved them from 'Popery, brass money and wooden shoes'. On 10 July 1690 William issued a proclamation setting the exchange rate at one crown for one old penny.

James has frequently been accused of acting in a cowardly fashion at the Boyne but it is not a fair assessment. He had intended to fight and was prepared to do so but was outmanoeuvred by William.

A much repeated story concerning James' flight has him saying to Lady Tyrconnell, 'Your countrymen can run well, madame', to which she replied, 'Not as well as your majesty, for I see you have won the race.' There is no contemporary record of this exchange and it seems to have been invented later.

Although the battle of the Boyne is the most famous and also the biggest battle fought in Ireland since Kinsale in 1601, it was not a single ferocious encounter confined to one battlefield but was instead a whole series of encounters spread over a wide area.

James Flees to France

The next morning James left at 5 a.m. with his horse guards for Wexford. At Bray, just south of Dublin, having crossed the River Dargle, James rather strangely ordered most of his guards to remain at the bridge and guard it until midday. The king and his party eventually reached Duncannon in County Wexford and took a boat from there to Kinsale and on to Dover in the south of England. He left there for France where he remained for the rest of his life as a guest of King Louis.

William Arrives Victorious in Dublin

During the battle of the Boyne the gates of Dublin were closed and the citizens were not allowed out of the city, while Protestants were ordered to stay indoors for the day. After the battle many of the defeated soldiers made their way back to Dublin and by nightfall the city was filled with weary, exhausted soldiers.

The victorious Williamite army made its way to Dublin after the battle and camped on the common in Crumlin. On 16 July William rode into the city to a rapturous reception from the Protestant population, who showered the soldiers with flowers and gifts and even hugged their horses. One account describes how 'they ran about shouting and embracing one another and blessing God for His wonderful deliverance. The poor Roman Catholics [were] now lying in the same terror as we had done some days before.'

After the battle of the Boyne Patrick Sarsfield is supposed to have said to one Williamite officer 'Change leaders and we will fight you all over again.'

When William's army made their way to Dublin after the Battle of the Boyne they brought with them the body of the great old soldier, the Duke of Schomberg, who had been killed in the battle. His body was later interred in St Patrick's Cathedral. The inscription on the stone later erected to his memory was composed by Dean Swift in 1730.

After the battle of the Boyne hordes of defeated soldiers roamed throughout the country. They burned and ransacked the homes of the gentry and among those was the home of William Edmundson in Mountmellick, County Laois. Edmundson was a Quaker who had come to Ireland with Cromwell and was a very brave man. He refused to wear a blindfold as the raiders prepared to shoot him and his three sons, saying that he wanted to look into their eyes as they killed him. Luckily one of the local leaders named Dunne stepped in and stopped the killing. Then in a final vindictive act, Edmundson's wife was stripped naked and thrown out on the road. The poor woman died later from exposure.

The SIEGE of LIMERICK
(August–September 1690)

The Williamites Look to Athlone

Shortly after the defeat at the Boyne, King James left Ireland and made his way to France. Lord Talbot (Tyrconnell) was then in command of the Jacobite forces with Patrick Sarsfield as the leading officer. They decided to make the River Shannon as their line of defence, concentrating their forces at Athlone and Limerick.

William then sent an army under General James Douglas, who had commanded a force at the Boyne, to take Athlone. The objective was to secure the bridge over the Shannon.

The garrison of the town of Athlone was commanded by a tough old soldier called Colonel Richard Grace, who had fought against Cromwell and had also served abroad in Spain.

Douglas and his army arrived outside the walls of Athlone on 17 July 1690 and called on Grace to surrender. In reply Grace fired his pistol in the air and said, 'These are my terms;

Colonel Richard Grace had previously adopted an unusual tactic when in command of the defence of Gerona in Spain which was being besieged by the French. He simply led his Irish regiment out towards the besiegers and joined them!

The civilian population of Ireland suffered terribly during the hostilities between the Jacobites and Williamites. One Williamite officer wrote at the time,

> These wretches came flocking in great numbers about our camp devouring all the filth they could meet with. Our dead horses crawling with vermin, as the sun had parched them, were delicious food to them; while their infants sucked those carcasses with as much eagerness, as if they were at their mothers' breasts.

The Williamite armies dreaded the attacks of the Irish guerrillas known as rapparees, who got their name from *rapaire*, the Irish name for a half-pike. The rapparees worked in small groups which could melt into the local population at will. One Williamite writer described them thus,

> When the rapparees have no mind to show themselves upon the bogs they commonly sink down between two or three little hills, grown over with long grass, so that you may as soon find a hare as one of them. They conceal their arms thus: they take off the lock and put it in their pocket or hide it in some dry place; they stop the muzzle close with a cork, and the touch-hole with a small quill, and then throw the piece itself into a running water or a pond; you may search till you are weary before you find one gun, but yet when they have a mind to mischief, they can all be ready in an hour's warning, for every one knows where to go to fetch his own arms, though you do not.

these only will I give or receive and when my provisions are consumed I will defend until I eat my old boots.'

The Irish regarded Athlone as a very important town because of its strategic position and Lord Deputy Tyrconnell ordered Sarsfield to bring reinforcements to defend it. (With the departure of King James, Tyrconnell was again in charge, with Sarsfield as the leading Jacobite officer.) Sarsfield collected a force of 500 cavalry and set out from Limerick on 28 July. Following behind the cavalry were four cannon guns and an escort of dragoons.

Before Sarsfield reached Athlone, however, the siege was over. Douglas had simply run out of ammunition and was worried about rumours that Sarsfield's army would soon be arriving. He would then have been caught between Grace's garrison and Sarsfield's army, so he did the sensible thing and marched southwards to join King William who was leading the rest of the army towards Limerick. They met up on the road between Tipperary and Limerick.

King William took the failure at Athlone in his stride because he planned to take Limerick and he would need as many men as possible. Once he had taken Limerick it would then be much easier to attack Athlone again and take it.

The Williamite Army Arrives at Limerick

As William approached Limerick he was shocked to find that the retreating Irish troops were adopting a 'scorched earth' policy of destroying houses, crops and barns. They also blocked roads to delay the advance of his army.

By 8 August 1690 the vanguard of William's army chased a group of Irish soldiers into the town and the main body of troops took up position on Singland Hill which lay to the southeast and which overlooked the city. The king sent a

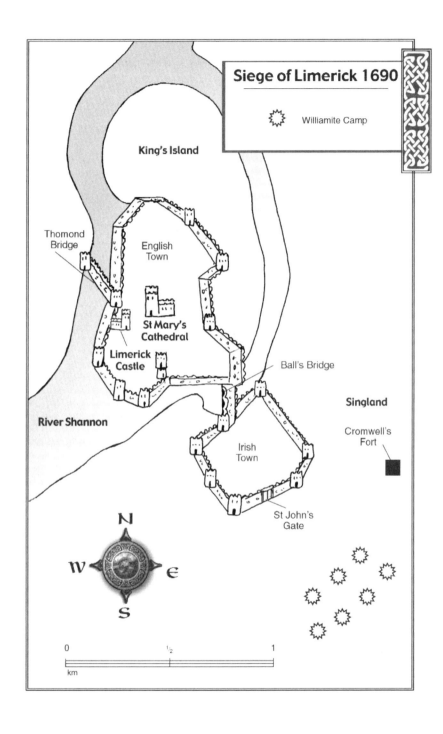

Siege of Limerick 1690

Williamite Camp

King's Island

Thomond Bridge

English Town

St Mary's Cathedral

Limerick Castle

Ball's Bridge

Singland

Cromwell's Fort

River Shannon

Irish Town

St John's Gate

N

W   E

S

0   ½   1
km

trumpeter to the city to send out delegates to negotiate the terms of surrender but this was rejected immediately by de Boisseleau, the French commander of the garrison.

Limerick at that time consisted of English Town on King's Island on the Shannon and Irish Town which lay on the southern bank of the river. English Town was connected to County Clare by Thomond Bridge and to Irish Town by Ball's Bridge. Both towns were walled. Although William's army had arrived at Limerick he could not commence the attack because his siege train, which could not travel as fast as his troops, was only then at Cashel in Tipperary.

'Sarsfield's Ride'

Just after the siege began a Williamite deserter came into the Irish camp with the information that William's siege train was on its way from Cashel. Sarsfield immediately assembled a body of 500 cavalry and set out to intercept it.

Patrick Sarsfield was over six feet tall and was a descendant of one of the Normans who had come to Ireland with Henry II in the twelfth century.

That same day, 11 August, a local Protestant landowner, Manus O'Brien, entered the Williamite camp and told them that a large body of Irish cavalry had crossed the Shannon at Killaloe. No one believed him but as O'Brien kept insisting that he had actually seen the Irish cavalry he was taken to William himself. He, too, was sceptical but he did send a Huguenot cavalry sergeant and a patrol to Killaloe to have a look. The sergeant found plenty of evidence to confirm the report and rode back to camp as fast as he could with the news. King William was still busy organising the siege but he gave an order that the matter should be seen to, and eventually Sir John Lanier was told to deal with it. Lanier took his time; although he got his orders on the morning of Monday 11 August, by afternoon he was still preparing.

Meanwhile the two-mile siege train wound its way slowly and noisily through the countryside from Cashel towards Tipperary. The day was hot and dry and the huge wagon-train raised clouds of dust as it moved along. It slowly passed through the village of Cullen and as evening fell it halted beside the ruins of Ballyneety Castle, sixteen kilometres from the Williamite camp.

By this time Sarsfield and his cavalry had ridden from Limerick to Killaloe and then on to Keeper Hill near the Silvermine Mountains where they hid during daylight on 11 August. That night they were guided by the famous Irish rapparee 'Galloping' Hogan to where the siege train escort was resting at Ballyneety. As the Irish party watched their target they were alarmed to see six troops of enemy cavalry approaching the camp on the Limerick road but to their great relief the troops passed by the siege train on their way to another escort duty.

In the darkness of 11 August Sarsfield led his men down

from the hills towards the enemy camp. The siege train consisted of more than 100 carts and wagons and eight eight-kilogram guns. The only soldiers nearby were twelve fusiliers and a few artillerymen. Eighty cavalry troopers had settled down for the night some distance away.

Their commanding officer, Captain Thomas Poultney, had not even patrols guarding the approaches to the camp. The ten guards who were on duty were only watching over the horses. It seems Poultney felt that they would be quite safe as they were only sixteen kilometres from William's camp.

While a body of 500 horsemen could not depend on the element of surprise, tradition has it that the Irish cavalry had learned that the password for the night was, by a strange coincidence, the name 'Sarsfield'! When challenged by one of the guards for the password the reply was 'Sarsfield is the word and Sarsfield is the man!'

Although Poultney tried to organise a resistance it was a hopeless task – Sarsfield and his men swept through the camp firing their guns and slashing with their sabres at anything that moved. The fighting was over in minutes and any wagoners and escorts still alive had fled.

Then Sarsfield ordered his men to burn everything. They gathered together huge quantities of gunpowder, bombs, cannonballs, matches, carbines, spikes, picks and spades and piled them all in a heap and set fire to them. Up to 100 wagons were burned and 120 barrels of gunpowder joined the fire. A large supply of food and stores was also needlessly destroyed. The bottoms of the pontoons were smashed open and then they turned to deal with the most important prize of all – the eight cannon.

These were packed with gunpowder, their muzzles stuck in the ground and a trail of powder laid to each one in turn. The

King William was very severe against looting: 'The king is very strict and will suffer none to plunder, so that this part of the army will be very poor because we are forced to be honest.' Anyone caught looting was hanged by the roadside as a deterrent to others.

On one occasion William was so angry with a soldier who had robbed an old Irishwoman that he beat the offender with his cane and then ordered him to be hanged.

When Sarsfield attacked William's siege train, he was intent on making prisoner the Dutch engineer, Willem Meesters, who was responsible for the guns. Meesters escaped by hiding in a bed of nettles until the raid was over.

A strange irony of the raid on the siege train was that the money wagon was not discovered by the raiders. As one of the Williamite officers reported,

> The money wagon was not touched by the enemy, but some of our own men, as I believe, took out some of the bags. The rest were secured.

whole lot was then blown sky-high in a tremendous explosion that could be heard miles away. The raiders then looted everything they could find in the camp. Lanier and his party heard the explosions when they were still a good distance from Ballyneety and they knew that they were too late to protect the siege train.

While Ballyneety was a serious blow to William it did not end the siege of Limerick and it was later found that six out of the eight guns could be salvaged. The barrels of two of the eight cannon had been split but the remaining guns had been blown from the pile, some relatively unscathed. Although the undercarriages were destroyed the guns could still be used.

Seven of the ten artillery guards were killed and thirteen other military personnel lost their lives and there were several casualties among the civilians who accompanied the train.

Preparing for the Siege

Meanwhile King William and his generals were busy preparing for the siege. They were within cannon shot of the walls, with their lines extended in a curve south and east of the city. The Limerick defences were in such a poor state that the French General Lauzun was appalled, declaring that 'the walls could be taken with roasted apples'. The elderly Tyrconnell agreed with him and they both recommended surrendering the city. Sarsfield would not hear of it and, together with a Frenchman, Captain Boileau, organised the soldiers and the remaining citizens in repairing the walls, towers and forts. Later Tyrconnell and Lauzun withdrew from the city to Galway, taking the French troops with them.

The badly armed defenders numbered about 25,000 men while William's well-equipped army numbered about 26,000. While at first the attackers were heartened by the departure

General de Boisseleau, the French commander of the Limerick garrison, was a tough forty-year-old and had spent over twenty-two years in the French army. He had plenty of siege experience in several European cities but he was not popular with his subordinates who did not trust him.

When one spot in Limerick's wall showed signs of crumbling under the Williamite bombardment Captain Boileau ordered huge sacks of wool to be hung over the spot to deaden the effect of the cannonballs. It did not seem to work, however, as the gunners managed to breach the wall.

The heroic resistance of the Limerick women is legendary. An on-the-spot Danish report says,

> The very women, prone as they are to violent passions, have since become furious. It is noticed that during the attack . . . they caused as much, indeed more, damage than the garrison by throwing huge stones on the assailants of whom a great number thus perished.

Less than two years after the surrender at Limerick Patrick Sarsfield was fatally wounded at the Battle of Landen in the Netherlands. As he lay on the ground, seeing his hands covered with blood from his wounds, he is said to have exclaimed, 'Would that this were shed for Ireland.'

of the French, they were dismayed some time later when news of the disaster at Ballyneety reached them. Still, after a delay of about a week, on 18 August 1690, William started the attack. He had got two large guns from Waterford and together with the cannon that survived the Ballyneety explosion he felt quite adequately equipped.

The Siege Begins

The action started with the attackers digging trenches towards the walls while the defenders did everything to hinder them by shooting at the sappers from a number of towers on the walls. When William's big guns were in position they opened up and soon levelled the towers. They then concentrated on a spot near St John's Gate to make a breach.

Cromwell's Fort, just outside the walls between St John's Gate and William's army, still remained in Sarsfield's hands, however, and provided strong resistance. Eventually the fort was stormed by the attackers and the garrison was forced to retreat within the city, leaving the fort to the Williamites. Then a wide breach was made in the city walls and the attacking army poured through, only to be met with ferocious resistance by the defenders.

One of William's foreign regiments, the Prussian Brandenburgs, forced their way right up to the Black Battery, one of the city's main batteries, which was placed over a vault used for storing gunpowder. During the fierce battle for the gun the vault beneath exploded with a roar and blew defenders, attackers, battery and everything else above it, to fragments.

Then Tyrconnell's son, Colonel Talbot, led a regiment of dragoons out through St John's Gate and, bravely running the gauntlet of the attacking troops, got to the breach and attacked the intruders from the rear. At the same time de Boisseleau's men mounted another frontal attack. The surviving Williamites had had enough and broke and ran.

The battle raged for nearly four hours and one eyewitness recorded,

> There was one continued fire of both great and small shot without intermission: insomuch that the smoke reached in one continuous cloud to the top of the mountain at least six miles off.

William Agrees to Abandon the Siege

William was very depressed with the great number of casualties he had suffered and the lack of success. To add to his worries the weather turned extremely bad and the trenches were filling with water. His losses were greater than at the Boyne – about 3,000 men, including some of his best troops and a great number of his officers. The Irish had only lost 400 men at most. At a council of war William wanted to continue the attack, even offering to lead it himself, but his officers voted against it. In the end William decided to abandon the siege on 29 August and the next day took the road to Waterford, from where he returned to England a frustrated and disappointed man.

The SIEGE of CORK
(September 1690)

Marlborough Brings his Army to Ireland

When William of Orange first arrived in England from Holland in November 1688 at the invitation of the Protestants he brought with him a large army of Dutch troops, leaving Queen Mary in charge of affairs with John Churchill, Duke of Marlborough, as military advisor. Later when Marlborough returned to England he found that William was in Ireland and having difficulties in laying siege to Limerick.

Marlborough proposed that his army of 5,000 men should sail to Ireland and take the ports of Cork and Kinsale to prevent them falling into the hands of the French should they decide to intervene. The proposal was not received with favour by the English council but Queen Mary referred the matter to William. He agreed on condition that Marlborough brought his own guns and arms as William could not spare any of his.

The arrival in Cork of the Duke of Würrtemberg led to a dispute with the Duke of Marlborough about whom should be in command. Each of them wanted to be in charge but they eventually agreed that they would be in command on alternate days. Although Marlborough tried to ease the tension between them by choosing 'Würrtemberg' as the password, there was always some tension and disagreement between the two commanders and the English and continental troops.

When tensions arose in England in 1688 at the birth of a son and heir to the Catholic Queen Mary, wife of James, Parliament thought it necessary to recall Protestant troops from Holland in case of trouble. So few actually returned that only three new regiments were formed in England and one of these was an Irish one. It was under the command of Colonel Roger McElligott, a Kerryman who had had charge of one of the regiments in Holland.

His regiment in England was based in Portsmouth and it soon became the terror of the town. The soldiers behaved disgracefully, robbing, getting drunk and beating up the inhabitants. One soldier created a riot by shooting into a Protestant church. The citizens of the city had given £500 to McElligott on the understanding that the suburbs would be spared but his promise was obviously not honoured.

Marlborough finally set sail with a fleet of eighty-two ships on 17 September 1690 and arrived in Cork a few days later. He was joined there by the Duke of Würrtemberg with 5,000 Danes, Dutch and Huguenot veterans of the Boyne, and the Dutch Major General Schravemoer with a force of Dutch and Danish cavalry and dragoons.

Cork Gets Ready

Cork was the largest town still in Jacobite hands and the second largest in Ireland. It was a walled town but being on an island in the River Lee it had the disadvantage that it was overlooked from the high ground on both sides of the river. The northern approaches to the city were defended by Shandon Castle and two newer forts. On the south side of the city was Elizabeth Fort and a hill called The Cat. Shortly before Marlborough's arrival the Jacobites had started to construct an outpost there, called Cat Fort. Most of the city's guns were located in Elizabeth Fort which meant that the walls were not adequately defended.

The walled city of Cork was about 800 metres by 300 metres. Three gates were in the walls, one in the north wall, one in the south wall and the third was a water gate which could admit small ships in the east wall. The northern and southern gates were connected to the mainland by bridges.

The commander of the city garrison of 4,500 men was Colonel Roger McElligott, who had rather tamely surrendered Waterford to William a short time previously. The defences were in a terrible condition. The ancient walls were crumbling and the cannon were totally inadequate. A single battery on the eastern side and a redoubt at Haulbowline were the main defences of the outer harbour.

The Siege Begins

The attack began simultaneously on both sides of the river on 22 September 1690. On the north side a brief shelling of Shandon Castle soon resulted in the abandonment of the castle by its garrison which retired into the city, burning the suburbs as they went.

Marlborough's fleet had entered the harbour on 22 September and quickly silenced the Jacobite battery. The next day his troops were on shore and moving towards the city and when they reached 'within a cannon shot of Cat Fort' they halted. Marlborough called on McElligott to surrender but the request was rejected out of hand and a 'bloody flag' was unfurled. The attackers exchanged some fire with the city but during the night the garrison abandoned the fort and it was soon occupied by English troops. Now Cork was open to batteries on the high ground on both sides of the city and when the steeple of St Finbarr's Cathedral was occupied by a Lieutenant Townsend and a small party of troops they caused havoc among the city's garrison.

There were two troops of Irish dragoons between the attackers and the city but they too retired to the safety of the walls after being shelled by field pieces. The dragoons set fire to the suburbs as they went and offered some resistance to the advancing troops but soon Marlborough's army was within a mile of the city, where they camped for the night. The next morning, 25 September, the attack resumed and Marlborough then chose Red Abbey as his headquarters. The rest of the day was spent in shelling the city.

On the north side the vacated Shandon Castle was occupied by General Schravemoer's troops, and some field pieces were put in position there. These constantly shelled the city during the siege. When Schravemoer called on the garrison to surrender McElligott 'sent back a very impertinent answer' to the effect that he was not frightened of Schravemoer's cavalry or Marlborough's infantry and was 'ready to receive them as soon as they pleased'.

Terms of Surrender are Discussed

During the night of 27 September McElligott allowed all the Protestants in the city to leave and wrote to Marlborough and Würrtemberg asking them to discuss terms of surrender. In reply Marlborough said that the whole garrison would be made prisoners of war, while Würrtemberg said they could march away if they laid down their arms. The matter never came to a decision because McElligott said he would accept neither set of terms.

On the morning of 28 September the Williamite guns continued their bombardment and made a breach in the walls. That afternoon the regiments of Marlborough and Würrtemberg launched an assault from both sides of the river over the marshy ground and waterways, the men wading up to their shoulders in water in some cases. The fleet also joined in the attack by shelling the city and concentrating fire on the breach in the wall. Two hours later the storming party reached a trench just thirty metres from the walls and were about to launch the final attack when McElligott asked for a parley but was again told that his men would be treated as prisoners of war. He would not accept this at first and the attack continued. Then he changed his mind and accepted the terms. Elizabeth Fort was to be handed over within the hour and the city gates thrown open the next morning.

The inhabitants were very badly treated by 'many seamen and other loose persons' entering through the breach and plundering the city before order was restored. McElligott

During the seventeenth century priests were forbidden to drink whiskey in public or attend fairs or markets. They were not allowed to take a female with them on horseback, even if the female was a relative.

Although the present-day image of the Quakers is of extremely gentle people, in the seventeenth century they were very intolerant of the Catholic religion. There was an incident in 1669 where a Quaker entered a Catholic church during a Mass while stripped to the waist and carrying a dish of burning coals on his head. He then proceeded to denounce the congregation for their idolatry. He was arrested and imprisoned for his actions.

A strange sport was practised in Cork at the time. Men would volunteer to be tossed in blankets for a fee of half a crown. In some cases it led to the death of the volunteer.

A traveller discovered that the women of the countryside used to wash their hair in stale urine and ashes to make their hair turn blonde. They then removed the smell by washing it in cold water.

barely escaped being murdered and the garrison were kept under guard for weeks. They were so denied food that they had to resort to eating dead horses. They were afterward imprisoned in very unsanitary conditions in gaols, houses and churches, while many of the soldiers were shot by a Captain Lauder on a 'death march' to Clonmel.

The attackers lost only 100 men in the siege and it later emerged that McElligott had almost no ammunition left. This information was known to the attackers through the Protestants who had been allowed to leave the city.

The SIEGE of KINSALE
(October 1690)

The Siege of Kinsale Follows Cork

No sooner had Cork been taken than the Williamite army turned its attention to Kinsale, twenty-seven kilometres away, which also occupied an important strategic position. It was again agreed that Marlborough and Würrtemberg should share the command on alternate days as they had done at Cork. Although the town had not got a defensive wall the harbour at the mouth of the Bandon was protected by two strong forts one on each side. The Old (James) Fort was on a spit of land overlooking the town and the New (Charles) Fort on the eastern bank. These were commanded by Sir Edward Scott who had weakened his forces by sending two regiments to the defence of Cork and now had no more than 2,000 men at his command. Marlborough dispatched a force of 500 cavalry under Colonel Villiers to seize the town on 29 September but when they called on Scott to surrender he threatened to hang the messenger. He ordered that the town should be burned but the order was not carried out before the Williamites overran the defences and managed to save many of the houses which afforded shelter for the men in the stormy autumn weather. The garrison and the town's inhabitants fled to the two forts and when these were called on to surrender they again ran up the blood-red flags of resistance.

The Williamites Arrive

The main Williamite army arrived on 2 October and it was decided to attack James Fort first. That night Major General Tettau led 600 fusiliers and 200 grenadiers to Innishannon where he crossed the Bandon by boat and made a surprise attack on the fort. After some fierce resistance, the 400 strong Irish garrison had to retire to the centre of the fort where they continued to resist for a time. They were forced to surrender, however, when some casks of gunpowder exploded and killed the fort's commander, Colonel O'Driscoll, and forty defenders.

With the fall of James Fort the commander of Charles Fort was called on to surrender but Colonel Scott, who had a garrison of 1,200, men replied that it would be time enough to talk about that in a month's time. Charles Fort was in a much better condition to resist: it had very good seaward defences and the land defences were strong enough to resist most attacks. The fort was roughly five-sided and surrounded by a deep dry moat which had only one well-defended drawbridge and gateway. There were five strong bastions and these were well equipped with guns. (A bastion was a projecting stone 'balcony' built on the walls of forts to allow defenders to fire along the walls at attacking troops.) The fort had two weak points, however: it was overlooked by high ground on the south and by Camp Hill on the southwest.

The Siege Begins

On 3 October 1690 William began the siege by directing Major-General Tettau, a skilled German engineer, to dig trenches to the southwest. The garrison made a sortie to prevent the work but were repulsed by the Williamite cavalry. Meanwhile efforts to bring cannon from Cork by sea were prevented by contrary winds so the besiegers were forced to bring them by land. The Williamite officers volunteered the services of their own horses and wagons for the task.

Six eleven-kilogram guns and two mortars arrived on 11 October and by the next morning were in position for attacking the fort. The big guns were in the Dutch sector on the high ground to the south of the Charles bastion and the two mortars were in the English sector to the southeast of the fort. The guns directed heavy fire on the citadel with devastating effect – many of the fort's guns were put out of action and a breach began to appear in the wall between the Flagstaff and Charles bastions. The bombardment increased the next day with the arrival of two more big guns. Things did not go smoothly all the time for the attackers, however, as the two mortars in the English sector ran out of ammunition, and fire from the fort forced the English troops to withdraw.

The End of the Siege

The bombardment continued and when a large breach was made in the wall by 15 October the garrison knew they had lost and they sought a parley. Honourable terms were agreed that stipulated that 'the fort be handed over intact, that the garrison bring away only their horses and baggage, that the officers retain their swords, and that both garrison and Catholic inhabitants have safe conduct to some place of security.' The garrison, numbering 1,000 men and led by Colonel Scott, marched out through the breach the next day and proceeded to Limerick.

When Marlborough entered the fort he found ninety-four guns, of which thirty-four were brass and, having appointed his brother, Brigadier Henry Churchill, as governor, he set sail for Portsmouth and home.

The Siege of Athlone
(June 1691)

Aid Arrives from France

By the end of 1690 Richard Talbot, now Duke of Tyrconnell, had gone to France to get assistance for the Jacobite cause and to ask for a military leader qualified to take over in Ireland. The following January he returned with some money and material for the Jacobite cause and with the promise of more assistance to come. On 8 May, 1691, a French expedition sailed up the Shannon with provisions and stores, but no money and no men. However, there was a French Major General on board, Charles Chalmont, Marquis de Saint-Ruth, with orders to take control of the Jacobite army. Saint-Ruth was a brave, experienced and competent soldier but very conceited. His arrival did little to ease the disharmony among the Jacobites but he was accepted as commander of the forces. He was accompanied by de Tessé and d'Usson (two officers who held the French equivalent

Commenting on Saint Ruth's arrival William sarcastically remarked that 'it was like pouring brandy down the throat of a dying man'.

Saint-Ruth declared that Ginkel deserved to be hanged for attempting to take Athlone which had such a strong army defending it, and that he himself should be hanged if he should allow it to happen.

The entire Jacobite artillery consisted of just seven brass six-pounder guns.

When the Irish troops arrived on the west bank of the Shannon at Athlone they could see the Williamite soldiers on the opposite bank. They spent the night of 22 June 'in pleasant raillery' with the enemy on the other side.

The next day saw the guards on both sides engaged in friendly conversation until a Williamite general put a stop to it.

rank of Lieutenant General) and some other lower-ranking officers. No troops were supplied, however, to assist the hard-pressed Irish.

Athlone Under Attack Again

After the failure at Limerick William had departed to England leaving General Ginkel in charge of his army. Ginkel now decided to make Athlone his next main objective and on 19 June, 1691, his army of 18,000 men appeared before the town. The main body of the Irish troops was encamped on the Connacht side, about a mile to the west of the town.

The walls, which had resisted the efforts of Douglas the previous year, were no match for Ginkel's heavy guns and soon a large breach was made. The breach was defended by 400 Irish troops but Ginkel threw 4,000 men into the attack and gradually the defenders were forced back. They retired over the Shannon bridge having lost half their number and left the eastern part of town to Ginkel's men.

That same evening Saint-Ruth arrived to take command of the Irish army. He ordered that earthen works should be constructed along the west bank of the river and placed his men behind these and in Athlone Castle. The Irish troops still controlled the greater part of the bridge which connected the English Town on the east side to the Irish Town on the west side. The bridge was constructed of stone but at the western end of it there was an arch and drawbridge, both made of wood. These wooden structures were soon destroyed by the Irish troops.

Saint-Ruth had brought an army of 16,000 foot, 3,000 horse and 2,000 dragoons and set up camp on a ridge three kilometres to the west of Athlone. He put Lieutenant General d'Usson in charge of the town and ordered that

The bombardment of the Jacobite lines was so fierce that Colonel Felix O'Neill of the defenders said, 'A cat could scarce appear without being knocked on the head by great or small shot.'

The army besieging Athlone was so short of provisions that the troops took to stealing to get food. Even then the food was not easily got, according to a Williamite chronicler, as the Irish rapparees 'have stripped the whole country of all the sheep and cattle so that we are like to have no provisions but what we have out of the stores'.

By 27 June up to thirty-two heavy cannon and six mortars were shelling west Athlone night and day. The gunners were given extra money and hogsheads of beer to encourage them in their efforts.

relays of regiments should take turns in the defence. D'Usson would have preferred a constant garrison but Saint-Ruth's idea was to get as many men as possible to experience active service. (It turned out that his decision was to prove disastrous.)

The Siege Begins

Ginkel started the bombardment on 21 June and it continued for ten days. In all, over 12,000 cannonballs were fired, as were 600 bombs and tons of stones thrown by the mortars.

By 23 June Athlone Castle was in ruins and a large breach had appeared in the town walls. But the bombardment continued. Irish Town was mostly reduced to rubble but William's troops could not cross the damaged bridge nor use pontoons to cross the river because of heavy fire from the Irish troops. Proposals to cross the Shannon further downstream were overruled by Ginkel who had a tendency to take too many opinions into consideration. He did give approval to an attempt to cross at a point a short distance upstream where the river was reported to be fordable. The reconnoitring party were ordered to return as soon as they had tested the ford but the lieutenant in charge could not resist the temptation to do a bit of cattle rustling and the Jacobites soon knew what was going on. They immediately erected strong earthen works on the opposite bank and that route was closed off.

The Bridge of Athlone

It was then decided to concentrate on the bridge. On 26 June the Williamites advanced 'inch by inch, as it were, the enemy sticking very close to it, though great numbers were slain by our guns.' They succeeded in reaching the end of the surviving portion of the bridge but there still remained a gap

During the crossing of the Shannon on 30 June one of the Williamite generals, Duke of Würrtemberg was carried across the Shannon on the shoulders of his grenadiers.

The twenty-four carpenters given the task of spanning the last missing section of the bridge were given a special payment for their dangerous task.

During the siege of Athlone Ginkel's thirty-two guns had used up nearly fifty tons of gunpowder, had fired twelve thousand cannonballs and six hundred bombs. As well as this the bombards had fired 'a great many tons of rocks'.

After the siege bodies were everywhere. 'One could not set his foot at the end of the bridge or castle, but on dead bodies, many lay buried under the rubble, and many not to be seen under the ruins, whereby the stink is insufferable.'

Athlone has the dubious distinction of being the most bombarded town in Great Britain and Ireland.

over the broken arch. On the night of 27 June the Williamites made strenuous efforts to repair the broken arch and the next morning, under heavy covering fire and sheltering behind fascines, they managed to bridge the gap with wooden beams and planks. (Fascines were tightly tied bundles of sticks, used to fill ditches or as a shelter against attack.)

A party of Williamite grenadiers were preparing to dash across and engage the enemy when a call was made on the Jacobite side for volunteers to destroy the bridge. Ten men carrying axes, led by Sergeant Costume, dashed forward and began hacking at the bridge. Within a minute they had all been shot dead but another party of twenty took their place. Eighteen of these were killed too but when the smoke cleared the planks were seen floating down the river.

Ginkel was desperate. He ordered another attempt to bridge the gap and throughout the day of 28 June the English pushed new fascines towards the gap under heavy covering fire from their gunners. The return fire from the defending Irish was too great however and the English were forced back off the bridge.

Ginkel now gave up hope of ever crossing the bridge and he knew that he had only two months before the onset of the autumnal rains in which to finish the campaign and take Galway, Limerick and Sligo. He decided on one last desperate gamble to cross the river by wading through it, and attack the Irish bridgehead from the western side and then repair the arch and drawbridge.

The Shannon is Crossed

A possible crossing point was selected a few hundred metres downstream from the bridge because some Irish soldiers had been seen crossing there. Three Danish soldiers, who were under sentence of death, were sent to test the ford and reported that, because of the hot dry summer, the water was only up to waist level and that there was room for twenty men marching abreast.

At about six o'clock in the evening of 30 June a volunteer party of Williamite grenadiers dashed into the river. The first party of sixty grenadiers wore heavy breastplates and waded in twenty abreast. They were closely followed by 1,500 more 'holding their fuses and bags of grenades above their heads'. The fire from the inexperienced Irish battalions was ragged and ineffective and the grenadiers got across successfully. As luck would have it, due to the foolish decision of Saint-Ruth to change the garrison each day, one of the most inexperienced regiments was on duty. It was composed of three infantry battalions, one of which had been raised as an unarmed labour battalion. The only action the men had been engaged in up to this was in stone-throwing during the siege of Limerick!

Once on dry land the grenadiers stormed along the bank to the town and the Irish defenders fled. D'Usson rushed to stop the retreat but was knocked out in the stampede and had to be carried unconscious to the camp. While the grenadiers attacked the defenders from the rear, the main body of the Williamite army advanced over the bridge. Quickly placing new planks over the gap, they raced across and soon Athlone was in Ginkel's hands.

The Williamite losses in the action were quite light: about thirteen killed and thirty-five wounded. On the Jacobite side it is thought 500 were killed on the final day and 1,200 during the whole siege.

The BATTLE of AUGHRIM
(July 1691)

Saint-Ruth Brings his Army to Ballinasloe

After the fall of Athlone Saint-Ruth took his army to Ballinasloe with no interference from the Williamite army. A council of war was held and Sarsfield put forward a plan to hold Limerick and Galway in strength, leaving the rest of Connacht open to the enemy forces, and then, when they had taken the bait, the Jacobites could cross the Shannon and devastate Leinster in Ginkel's rear and maybe even take Dublin. Most of the officers favoured the plan but Saint-Ruth was determined to give battle and had already chosen what he regarded as the perfect place – the high ground near Aughrim, about eight kilometres from Ballinasloe.

The Battle of Aughrim

The site was on the east slope of Kilcommodon Hill with a belt of bog along the front except for two narrow paved

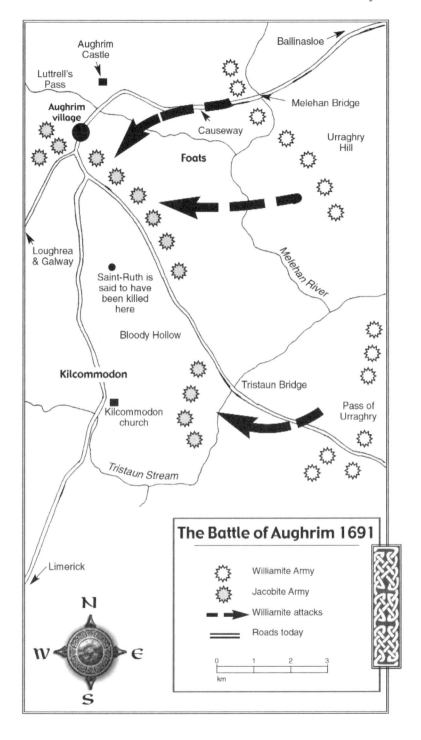

Aughrim
Castle

Luttrell's
Pass

Ballinasloe

**Aughrim
village**

Melehan Bridge

Causeway

Urraghry
Hill

Foats

Loughrea
& Galway

Saint-Ruth is
said to have
been killed
here

Melehan River

Bloody Hollow

Kilcommodon

Tristaun Bridge

Kilcommodon
church

Pass of
Urraghry

Tristaun Stream

Limerick

The Battle of Aughrim 1691

Williamite Army

Jacobite Army

Williamite attacks

Roads today

0   1   2   3
km

N
W   E
S

passes, one on the north of the bog and one on the south of it. The passes were so narrow that only two horsemen could ride abreast on them.

Saint-Ruth took up position on 8 July and so, in the event, had four days to get everything ready. He positioned his army between Kilcommodon Church on his right, and Aughrim Castle on his left. The army was extended along a line about three kilometres long. Some hedges and ditches on the lower slopes of Kilcommodon Hill were to be used as trenches and others were levelled to afford a clear line of fire towards the passes that led across the bog.

Saint-Ruth was convinced that he was the best general in the country and was confident that he could defeat Ginkel. He also had no wish to go back to Louis XIV after his failure at Athlone. The only reservation he had was the low morale of the Irish troops – he knew they blamed him for the defeat. He therefore tried to make himself popular with the troops and went out of his way to be 'very kind and familiar with the Irish officers whom he formerly treated with disrespect and contempt'. He also encouraged the clergy to instil religious fervour in the army. At Mass for the troops that day, a Sunday, the priests assured the men of a glorious victory and urged them to give no quarter to the enemy. The tactics worked, morale was high, deserters had begun to return and the troops were ready for battle.

At dawn on Sunday morning, 12 July, 1691, Ginkel's army of 20,000 men marched out of Ballinasloe on to the road to Aughrim. The scouts led Ginkel's general staff across country until they were about 500 metres from Kilcommodon Hill and when Ginkel used his field-glasses he could see the grey coats of the Jacobite soldiers. Saint-Ruth also had an army of 20,000 men but had only nine cannon to Ginkel's eighteen,

Saint-Ruth spoke no English and all his commands had to be translated for the men.

A copy of the rather extraordinary speech Saint-Ruth is said to have made to the troops before the battle was allegedly found on the dead body of his secretary. It read:

> Stand to it therefore, my dears, and bear no longer the reproaches of the heretics who brand you with cowardice, and you may be assured that King James will love and reward you, Louis the Great will protect you, all good Catholics will applaud you, I myself will command you, the church will pray for you, your posterity will bless you, God will make you all saints, and His holy mother will lay you in her bosom.

As Ginkel marched through the country to Aughrim he complained that the rapparees were burning all before him and they were so numerous that 'we can neither find forage nor cover, which hinders much our march'.

The course of the battle of Aughrim was rather confused and it is not easy to determine which of the various conflicting accounts is the most accurate.

but was so over-confident that he had made no effort to conceal his position. Scouts brought back the bad news to Ginkel that there was no way through the bog except the two places that were guarded by Jacobite soldiers: at the village of Aughrim, and across the ford the other side of Kilcommodon Hill at the southern end of the bog.

In fact Saint-Ruth had indeed picked a near perfect position. Although his poorly trained soldiers were vulnerable to cavalry attacks, the only way Ginkel's horse could do so was at these two places. Saint-Ruth placed a cavalry regiment at each of these two areas and spread his infantry on the hill between them. He intended to force the English to attack him full on; he knew they could not get through Aughrim on his left because it was approached by a narrow causeway and was dominated by Aughrim Castle. The only other approaches were across the ford on his right which was strongly guarded, and through the bog at his centre.

Saint-Ruth placed two infantry regiments guarding the causeway where they were well protected and concealed in trenches and ditches. Two commanders, John Hamilton and William Dorrington, were in command there but Saint-Ruth was in overall charge. He also placed one cavalry regiment, commanded by Lord Galmoy, behind the hill – it was the only reserve he could afford. He positioned his two remaining regiments, comprised mostly of dragoons and cavalry, on his flanks: the one on his right, commanded by Sarsfield, was to prevent the enemy crossing the ford, and that on his left, in the charge of Dominic Sheldon, was deployed around Aughrim Castle. The castle itself was occupied by Colonel Walter Burke who had 200 musketeers. Behind the castle on open ground were four dragoon regiments and behind them, four cavalry regiments.

The causeway at the approach to Aughrim was less than sixty metres long and only wide enough to allow two horsemen to ride abreast. Saint-Ruth had ordered the Jacobite officer Henry Luttrell to hold the pass with his cavalry, but for some reason Luttrell withdrew after 'some small resistance'. The story grew that Luttrell had been 'bought with filthy lucre'. Not long after Aughrim, Luttrell wrote to Ginkel and eventually received a Williamite pension.

Some people never forgave Luttrell and blamed him for the defeat at Aughrim. His family became very wealthy but in 1717 he was shot dead in his sedan chair in Dublin, not in revenge for Aughrim but by a jealous husband.

The way past Aughrim Castle is today is known locally as Luttrell's Pass.

The Battle Begins

The battle began in a rather haphazard way. As Ginkel's horsemen rode forward to inspect the lie of the land they came under fire from some of Sarsfield's cavalry patrols. Some skirmishing ensued and the Williamite horsemen had to call up reinforcements. Orders were then sent to them to hold off but, in spite of this, fighting increased and more squadrons were drawn into action. Firing continued until well after nightfall.

This was exactly what Saint-Ruth had wanted: the enemy was forced into action against his strongest position, that occupied by Sarsfield. Ginkel, on the other hand, had decided to attack Saint-Ruth's right flank in the hope of drawing some of the enemy away from Aughrim Castle on the other flank, so that his army could force their way through there.

The main Williamite advance began at 5 p.m. on 12 July 1691 and met with fierce resistance. The advance was led by Major General La Forest's Danish and Huguenot cavalry who found it very hard going over the bog with the sun in their faces. Riding close together the 1,500 men surged across the ford and up on the western bank, where they were immediately attacked by Sarsfield's men. It was the most serious cavalry battle of the war and the fast and furious fighting lasted for over an hour and a half. Soon the area around the ford was a mass of dead and dying men and horses. The Irish dragoons, who had long abandoned their horses, waded into the ford and fired at point-blank range at the advancing Williamites. Gradually the sheer numbers of the attackers forced the Irish back towards Sarsfield's position and there the attackers were halted by his second line of cavalry. The Williamites were in a difficult position: they

So many men were killed where the initial fighting took place that it is known today as Bloody Hollow

One of the Williamite officers later wrote:

> We on the right attacked them, they gave their fire and away they ran to the next ditches and we, scrambling over the first ditch, made after them to the next from where they gave us another scattering fire and away they ran to another ditch behind them . . . later in climbing these ditches and still following them from one to another, no man can imagine we could possibly keep our order, and here in this hurry there was no less than six battalions so intermingled that we were at a loss to know what to do.

Some of the Williamite cavalry carried bundles of large sticks with them to lay over the boggy ground to provide better footing for their horses.

could not go forward where they were exposed to cannon fire and the muskets of the dragoons and, with the bog flanking them on either side, it seemed the only course open was to retreat.

Meanwhile Major General Mackay, in the centre facing the bog, ordered his men forward and to establish a foothold on the other side. His men found the crossing to be a nightmare. Slipping, stumbling, and cursing, they waded through mud and water up to their waists, and those who managed to get through were immediately fired on by the Irish troops lying in wait behind the ditches. To the exhausted Williamites the enemy was often invisible. The English chronicler George Story wrote:

> Several were doubtful whether the Irish had any men in that place or not, but they were convinced of it at last, for no sooner were the Dutch and the rest got within twenty yards or less of the ditches that the Irish fired most furiously upon them.

Gradually the Williamite troops fought their way through the smoke and gunfire. They would reach the nearest ditch only to find that the Irish had retreated to the next one. All the time the Williamite troops were in full view of the enemy who wrought terrible damage on them. All was confusion: some of the officers ran forward, others tried to form order, others were still struggling through the mud. This process continued until eventually they reached the other side.

It was quite clear to the Williamite officers now that they could not remain where they were on the edge of the bog. Ignoring Mackay's orders, a commanding officer, Colonel Thomas Earle rallied his men and led them on until they became so exhausted that they could move no further. At this

Sleeping arrangements among the ordinary country folk were extremely primitive in the seventeenth century. One traveller noted:

> The floor is thickly strewn with fresh rushes and, stripping themselves entirely naked, the whole family lie down at once together, covering themselves with blankets if they have them and if not, with their day clothing; but they lie down decently and in order, the eldest daughter next the wall, furthest from the door, then all the sisters according to their ages. Next the mother, father, and sons in succession, and then the strangers, whether the travelling peddler, tailor or beggar. Thus the strangers are kept aloof from the female part of the family . . . there is great propriety of conduct.

The practice of bathing the whole body did not become general until the end of the seventeenth century, although swimming was common during the summer months.

A particular form of wrestling was common in the seventeenth century. Each man wore a leather belt round his waist; each took a grip of his opponent's belt and they would begin wrestling at a command.

The average wage of a labourer in 1676 was four pence a day.

Travel between Ireland and England was extremely hazardous in the seventeenth century. One man records having gone on board ship at Chester on 15 August, 1698, expecting to reach Ireland in two days, but having spent 'near seven week cast up and downe and putt in to five several harbours . . . every howre expecting the fate of a mercyless sea' finally reached Dublin on 25 September!

moment the waiting Irish troops charged, using their muskets as clubs and the only thing the weary English troops could do was to make their way as quickly as possible back down through the bog. The English attack had failed.

Things were not going any better at the ford. Major General La Forest's cavalry and dragoons made several attempts to break through Sarsfield's defences but were repulsed each time. After suffering heavy losses La Forest was also back where he started.

Saint-Ruth Senses Victory

Meanwhile Ginkel had ordered his infantry to make several attacks across the bog but these, too, ended in failure. The whole operation seemed to be a disaster. Saint-Ruth was so elated that he shouted to his officers, '*Le jour est a nous, mes enfants!*' ('The day is ours, my boys!')

Ginkel on the other hand was despondent at the lack of success – everything he tried seemed to fail. The only part of the army not yet committed was the English cavalry on his right. If they could get over the causeway and if the infantry could provide cover for them things might change. The failure of La Forest meant that the only open ground that might be reached by horse was on the other side of the causeway. Unfortunately the orders that Mackay had given to his troops to secure that end of the causeway had not been carried out. His men had been driven back and the Irish were in the same positions as before. There was one important difference now, however; before the battle Saint-Ruth had placed two regiments of foot at the causeway but these had been called upon to assist in the heavy fighting in the centre and had not been replaced since. Ginkel had noticed this and he now saw an opportunity.

He ordered the Marquis de Ruvigny, who had fought at Cork along with Marlborough, and was now in command on the right wing, to advance over the causeway. Two cavalry regiments, those of commanders Ruvigny and Villiers, immediately set off on the desperate mission. They had only six squadrons of cavalry and dragoons but if they got across successfully others could follow.

Mackay had also noticed the weakness and spoke to his cavalry officers about taking advantage of the situation. They were less than enthusiastic. They pointed out that they could not ride through the bog and that they did not know where the bog ended. Mackay then ordered an officer to check the route but he refused point-blank as he would be in open view of the gunners in Aughrim Castle.

Mackay was extremely angry and turned and set his horse at a low wall without having noticed that there was a bog on the other side of it. The horse cleared the wall but sank in the soft ground on landing and Mackay was thrown into a bog-hole. He climbed out covered in mud and soaking wet. If he had been angry before he was absolutely furious now and ordered his officers in no uncertain terms to get their men over the bog!

Aughrim Castle is Attacked

Aughrim Castle was defended by 200 musketeers under the command of Jacobite colonel, Walter Burke and he could see the English, less than forty metres away, crossing the causeway. He knew he had not enough fire-power to stop them completely but he intended reducing their ranks a good deal. As the enemy rode forward he gave the order to fire. The Williamite dragoons dismounted and returned heavy fire in an effort to keep the defenders below the parapet.

Firing continued at a furious rate but the garrison's supply of ammunition soon began to run low so it was decided to break open new supplies recently obtained. The musket balls were hurriedly handed out but then to their horror they found that the ammunition was for English muskets and was too large for their French flintlocks.

In desperation the men looked frantically for anything they could use. They tore the brass buttons off their uniforms, broke their ramrods into small pieces and even used small pebbles. The English cavalry and dragoons were surprised at how little resistance was offered as they swiftly charged forward. Then they got another pleasant surprise as they reached the open ground before the castle: the two Irish battalions had still not been replaced by Major-General Dorrington.

The castle fell to the Williamites shortly afterwards and most of the garrison were put to death. Only thirteen officers, including Colonel Burke and forty 'other ranks' were made prisoner. Ginkel was delighted at de Ruvigny's success but decided that he would need reinforcements to hold on, so he sent word to the cavalry facing Sarsfield to gallop over to Ruvigny's assistance.

The Death of Saint-Ruth

Saint-Ruth was surprised at the fall of the castle but he was not too alarmed as he felt that he had enough cavalry, not just to stop the intruders but to wipe them out. He sent word to Sheldon and Galmoy to charge the English squadrons. He was still elated at his success so far and he decided to gallop over to his left wing to witness what he hoped would be the greatest and most successful cavalry charge in the war. He called to his men, 'They are beaten, let us beat them to the

It is not known where Saint-Ruth was buried. Some think it was in Loughrea, while others say he was buried in the graveyard at Kilcommodon Church on Aughrim Hill and later removed by persons unknown.

The Irish soldiers fleeing from the battle threw away their muskets. Ginkel at first offered six pence per gun handed in but when he began to receive wagonloads of them he reduced the price to two pence.

For years after the battle of Aughrim many of the bones of the dead could still be seen on the ground. The English troops had refused to bury any of the dead except the bodies of their own comrades.

The battle of Aughrim was one of the bloodiest ever fought in Ireland. Among the dead after the battle were one general, three major generals, twenty-two colonels, seventeen lieutenants, and 7,000 rank and file.

purpose' and led his men down the hill. At that moment a single cannonball fired by Ginkel's men from the other side of the bog, struck him and 'carried off his head' and his lifeless body fell to the ground. A cloak was thrown over his body and he was carried back over the brow of the hill.

Without Saint-Ruth the Jacobites were paralysed. He had not told his second-in-command de Tessé, or any of his officers, what his plans were. The command of the army was taken over by de Tessé who did his best to retrieve the situation. It was all in vain – the Irish infantry were already running back up the hill to escape. Sarsfield, who had been the most successful leader in the battle was too far from Saint-Ruth's position to hear of his death but soon he could see with his own eyes that the Irish were falling back in every quarter but his own. He was faced with a terrible dilemma. He had only eight cavalry regiments against the whole English army. He knew he could not defeat them but he decided that he could delay their advance to allow the Irish infantry to escape. Again and again he charged and succeeded in preventing some of the English cavalry from joining the indiscriminate slaughter of the fleeing foot soldiers. An English account at the time says,

> Colonel Sarsfield, who commanded the enemy in their retreat, performed miracles, and if he was not killed or taken it was not from any fault of his.

The defeat at Aughrim was followed shortly afterwards by the surrender of Galway and Sligo under favourable terms and their garrisons were allowed to retire to Limerick. Ginkel next moved against that city and after a month's siege it surrendered. Then on 3 October 1691 the Treaty of Limerick was signed. The general terms of the treaty (which allowed freedom of religion and confirmed that Catholics who had sided with King James would retain possession of their lands) were soon shamefully broken by the Protestant ascendancy, and the enactment of the infamous Penal Laws soon followed.

The BATTLES of ARKLOW
(9 June 1798)
and
VINEGAR HILL
(21 June 1798)

The Society of United Irishmen

Towards the end of the eighteenth century the country was in a state of great unrest, mainly because of the outrageous behaviour of the government troops. A secret society called the United Irishmen was formed in 1791 by Theobald Wolfe Tone with the aims of reforming the Irish parliament (which supported the British government and only represented the Protestant population) and redressing the grievances of the people. The society spread rapidly throughout the country and five years later it is said to have had 50,000 members.

Although the aim of the society was to bring about change by peaceful means, by the end of the century they reluctantly concluded that the use of force was their only hope of achieving reform. Consequently they planned a rebellion which was to start in Dublin on 23 May 1798. But spies had

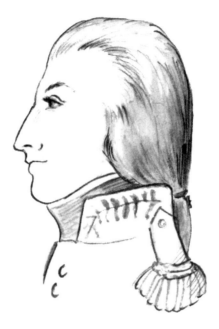

Theobold Wolfe Tone founded the Society of the United Irishmen in 1791.

revealed the plans to the government, which acted swiftly by arresting most of the leaders and the Dublin rebellion was aborted. The rising did go ahead in Wicklow, Wexford and Kildare, however, with some further activity in Meath, Offaly, Carlow and parts of County Dublin.

When the Wexford rising broke out on Whit Sunday, 27 May 1798 it was not the result of careful planning. In fact the United Irishmen organisation was relatively weak in the county. The rebellion was provoked by the outrageous behaviour of government troops such as the North Cork Militia over the previous months. This regiment roamed the county, searching for arms and torturing and killing suspects without mercy – twenty-eight suspected United Irishmen were shot dead in Ball Alley in Carnew and a further thirty-four in Dunlavin.

As late as Easter 1798 Father John Murphy, parish priest of Boolavogue near Enniscorthy, refused the sacraments to members of the United Irishmen who would not repudiate their secret oath and he also collected signatures of 750 of his parishioners for an address of loyalty to Lord Lieutenant Camden in an effort to stave off martial law.

By May however the activities of the Ferns Yeomanry and the North Cork Militia in the area were becoming intolerable; rumours of massacres were rife and the killings in Carnew and Dunlavin created panic. From this time onward Father Murphy openly threw in his lot with the United Irishmen, saying,

> Look to the inhuman slaughter in Carnew and, if the reported butchery in Dunlavin is true, it is worse. Our jails are full of the best of our people and it may be our lot to be in company with them before tomorrow night.

Membership of the United Irishmen was punishable by death. When the army authorities suspected that seventy members of the Monaghan Militia were members, commander-in-chief General Lake ordered that four privates who refused to inform on their comrades be executed beside their coffins. The rest of the troops were then ordered to file past to view the bodies.

A large number of Catholic priests were involved in the Wexford Rising.

A Carmelite, Father John Byrne, played an active part in the camps in the south of the county. He had a rather unfortunate death in 1799. He was visiting Clougheast Castle and when the owner thought Byrne was going to attack him he chased him out of the castle. As the friar was fleeing through the main door, the portcullis fell on him and killed him.

When the nephew of Father Thomas Clinch was killed by yeomen the priest joined the rebels. He cut a remarkable figure, being of huge stature, and rode a large white horse. He wore his vestments under his clothes and carried a scimitar on his broad crossed belt. During single combat on Vinegar Hill he was shot and wounded. Although he managed to ride away he died soon after.

Many of Colonel Walpole's troops fleeing from the battle at Tubberneering threw away their guns and turned their coats inside out so that they would not be recognised as soldiers.

Battle at the Hill of Oulart

When Father Murphy's church at Boolavogue was burned down by the members of the North Cork Militia he led a party of peasants against a detachment of 110 militia at the Hill of Oulart near Ferns on 27 May 1798. The rebels decisively defeated the militia and captured 800 muskets in the battle. They next marched on Enniscorthy which was defended by another force of militia. By driving a herd of cattle before them, the rebels broke through the defenders' lines and took the town after a four-hour battle. The defeated garrison and most of the Protestant population of the town fled to Wexford town. The garrison in Gorey then decided to abandon their position and left for Arklow, leaving Gorey undefended. Next, the insurgents set up camps at Carrigroe Hill near Ferns, on Carrickbyrne Hill between New Ross and Wexford, and on Vinegar Hill near Enniscorthy. On 1 June they marched from Carrigroe to take over Gorey but were routed by a force of yeomen under a Lieutenant Elliott. Gorey was then again garrisoned by government troops.

Arklow Abandoned by its Garrison

Later General Loftus led 1,500 men from Gorey to attack the Carrigroe camp but the rebels defeated one of his columns under Colonel Walpole at Tubberneering near Gorey by making good use of the hedges and other natural cover. About 110 of the troops were killed, and three cannon fell into the hands of the rebels. The remnants of Walpole's column and the Gorey garrison reached Arklow as darkness fell. The local commander there thought that the town could not be successfully defended, however, and he and his garrison and all the newcomers marched out the road to Wicklow town, abandoning Arklow to its fate.

Father Murphy of Boolavogue is described as being a 'well-built man of medium height, well fleshed, light complexioned, with a high forehead and receding hair over regular features'. He was very popular with his flock but was 'terrible when opposed'.

The exact date of the execution of John Kelly ('The Boy from Killann') is not known but his treatment was particularly gruesome. Badly wounded in the battle of New Ross when a bullet shattered his thigh, he was brought to the gallows on Wexford Bridge. After he was hanged his head was cut off and kicked through the streets of the town by the soldiers. Kelly's own sister was an unfortunate witness to the behaviour of the soldiers.

On 25 June 1798 Matthew Keogh, Father Roche and seven other men were taken to Wexford Bridge for execution. The makeshift gallows was a metal arch that spanned the bridge and the soldiers hanged the men by putting a rope around their neck and hauling them from the ground. The rope round Father Roche snapped the first time and he fell unconscious to the ground. When he recovered he was hauled up again and hanged. The bodies of the men were grossly mutilated after hanging and then thrown in the river. Because Keogh was a Protestant he was treated with great vindictiveness – his head was cut off, stuck on a pike and paraded around the town. Later it was left for months on a pike outside the courthouse.

The same treatment was given to the bodies of Bagenal Harvey and another leader called Cornelius Grogan after they were executed on the bridge on 28 June. Their heads were then placed alongside Keogh's outside the courthouse.

When the Arklow garrison and others reached Wicklow town the commander there was livid at their apparent cowardice. He immediately sent a small detachment of troops to Arklow to retake the town but these did not reach it until the next day. Consequently, Arklow was a full day without a garrison but the rebels seemed to be totally unaware of this.

The Rebellion Spreads

The defeat at Tubberneering filled the authorities with dread. Lord Lieutenant Camden asked for immediate reinforcements from England, saying, 'The salvation of Ireland, on which Great Britain as an empire eventually depends, requires that this rebellion be instantly suppressed'. Many Protestants fled from Dublin to England and when the news came that hostilities had started in Ulster the authorities in Dublin were extremely nervous. One man wrote to England saying, 'For God's sake urge them to send at once the strongest force they possibly can.'

The recently appointed commander-in-chief, General Gerard Lake, responded to the developments in Wexford by sending a force of about 1,000 men, led by Lieutenant General Francis Needham, towards Arklow on 5 June. On his way from Dublin Needham collected an additional 360 members of the Cavan Militia under Colonel Maxwell from the camp at Loughlinstown in South Dublin. The force, all that could be spared from the defence of Dublin, was put into commandeered carriages and reached Wicklow town the same evening where Needham learned of the abandonment of Arklow. Because it was night-time he decided to spend the night in Wicklow town and to start on the march again in the morning.

Fencibles were men who enlisted only for the duration of the war. They were completely raw and gained a reputation for 'the most wretched discipline'. Their officers showed 'the most dishonourable sentiments and ignorance'.

One young soldier defending Arklow wrote of the attacking Wexford men:

> At 4 o'clock . . . I saw in a moment thousands appear on the top of ditches, forming one great and regular circular line . . . as thick as they could stand. They all put their hats on their pikes and gave most dreadful yells. I could clearly distinguish their leaders riding through their ranks with flags flying.

Another defender also mentions the rebels' green and yellow flags of the rebellion and the flag that was to become a national emblem, the green flag with the harp and without the crown. He tells how one of the rebel officers rode out in front shouting, 'Blood and wounds, my boys! Come on, the town is ours!' A moment later a fusillade of musket fire brought down both horse and rider. When the rebel raised his head to look about him he was shot dead.

Lieutenant General Needham later wrote:

> The perseverance of the enemy was surprising and their efforts to possess themselves of the guns on my left were the most daring, advancing even to the muzzles, where they fell in great numbers.

On 6 June he marched to Arklow, occupied the barracks there and set up camp nearby for the rest of his troops. He then set his men to levelling ditches, digging trenches and erecting earthworks on the southern side of the town. Some pieces of artillery which his reinforcements had brought were put in position commanding the southern approaches also.

Then General Lake despatched an additional infantry troop of 480 Durham Fencibles, and later a regiment of the Dumbartonshire Fencibles, to Arklow and these reached the town on 9 June, the very day the battle started. The troops were given only enough time to eat the loaves of bread that Needham had ordered to be baked for them and 'had scarce thrown off their knapsacks' before being moved into the line. By this time Needham's makeshift army totalled about 2,000 troops and he proceeded to deploy them on the south side of the town in a crescent line about 800 metres long facing the oncoming rebels.

Needham was in a good position: his men were dug in, were well armed with light weapons and they had six cannon. His opponents, the rebels, were not military men at all, but just ordinary workers, peasants and farmers, who had been driven to rebellion by the activities of the authorities. Most of the rebels were armed with pikes, although there were about 2,000 firearms among them also. They had a few captured cannon as well but the rebels were so inexperienced with these weapons that most of the time they caused little damage.

This rag-taggle army, numbering about 8,000 men, now marched out of Gorey at ten o'clock in the morning of 9 June 1798 to lay siege to Arklow. It is not clear who exactly were the leaders – there seems to have been no single individual in overall charge – but among them were Anthony Perry, a

General Lake adopted a policy of terror in his dealing with the rebels and gave orders that no prisoners were to be taken.

The firearms carried by the insurgents were of every type available, muskets, fowling pieces, and even blunderbusses. Gunpowder and shot was always scarce. The powder was often carried loose in pockets or sometimes in small paper parcels. Many of the Wexford rebels were armed with pitchforks, billhooks, scythes, hay knives and any other farm implement that could be used in a battle.

One enterprising man from Wicklow, Joseph Holt, made his own gunpowder from sulphur, saltpetre and charcoal. He got the charcoal by burning heather.

prominent Protestant landowner, ex-yeoman and United Irishman Billy Byrne of Ballymanus in Wicklow and Esmond Kyan, who commanded the artillery. (Kyan had only one good arm, having had a forearm amputated before the rising.) Another leader, who was subsequently killed in the battle, was Father Michael Murphy of Ballycanew but he did not arrive until the battle was nearly over.

The marching companies did not keep a proper distance between each other and, since the roads were narrow, there was frequent crowding and confusion. Billy Byrne decided to try to enforce some order and set his horse to jump a hedge so that he could ride through the fields to the front. The horse fell, however, and threw him.

The day was extremely hot and dry, and the men had to be rested now and again. Consequently, it took nearly six hours to reach Arklow when it should have taken about three.

When the rebels came in sight of the town they were stopped by their leaders to decide on the best method of attack. The decision was to attack the town simultaneously in two large columns, one along the Coolgreany Road and the other along the Rock Road on the coast. The men attacking along the Coolgreany road had a distance of two miles to march while those on the Rock Road had only a mile and a half.

Ammunition Runs Out

Four hours after starting the attack on Arklow the rebels manning the cannon had little to show for their efforts. They had run out of ammunition and by eight o'clock in the evening they decided to withdraw.

Billy Byrne, who had earlier fallen from his horse, led a body of mounted Wicklowmen up the hill along the

The pikes used were of three different designs. Most of them had an iron or steel spike attached to the end of an ash staff which was between three and four metres long.

The second design was similar to the first but had a curved hook projecting sideways from the blade. This hook was useful in cutting a cavalryman's reins or saddle girth.

The third type was similar to the second but also had an axe head opposite the hook.

Whenever a pikeman could get his hands on an enemy musket he immediately abandoned his pike and became a 'musketeer' whether he knew how to use the gun or not.

A rebel leader in the battle of Arklow in 1798, General Anthony Perry, was a local liberal Protestant. He led a large force in the battle and organised it with such skill that 'it would not have dishonoured a more experienced veteran in arms'.

He was captured, beaten, his hair was cropped, gunpowder was rubbed on his head and then set alight. He survived, however, and did his utmost to restrain some of the wilder elements of his own troops. He was again arrested and was hanged on 12 July, 1798.

Father John Murphy was captured by yeomen in Tullow on 3 July 1798 and publicly flogged in the town square, hanged and then decapitated. His body was then thrown into a barrel of pitch and set on fire. His badly damaged body was secretly retrieved and buried at Mullawn cemetery outside Tullow.

Coolgreany Road to attack one of Needham's forward outposts. After some exchange of gunfire the defenders abandoned their position and retired to the town to alert the garrison.

Later the larger rebel force assigned to the same road surged along it and some of the fields alongside. It was then decided to send part of the force to join the other column attacking the town on the Rock Road. Neither force experienced much resistance on their march and by six o'clock a crescent of rebel forces stretched over 2000 metres in front of the town. The moment of decision had arrived; if Needham lost this battle the whole country might be lost to the rebels.

The first line of the town's defences on the west at the Coolgreany road, at a part known as the Fash, was manned by the Durhams and Dumbarton Fencibles. Needham had placed most of his cavalry on the east side at the Rock Road, with some units at the bridge and others behind the trenches. Some exchange of gunfire took place but soon the fencibles gave up their positions and fled back to the barricade.

Once in position in front of the town on the Coolgreany Road, the rebel cannons, directed by Kyan, started firing on the garrison and this marked the beginning of the battle. The first few salvoes missed their target because they were too high but after some adjustments the gunners managed to direct their fire on the defenders. Several soldiers were killed, a cannon was destroyed and one shot hit a stock of ammunition and blew it up.

The insurgent leaders were so encouraged by the sight of columns of smoke rising from behind the barricades that the order was given to attack and, with a huge cheer, about 6,000 men started across open ground towards the enemy lines.

A Protestant clergyman and contemporary historian, the Reverend James Gordon, described how the body of Father Michael Murphy was treated after his death:

> Some of the troops of the Ancient British regiment cut open the body of the dead Father Michael Murphy after the battle of Arklow, took out his heart, roasted his body, and oiled their boots with the grease which dropped from it.

Crowds of women and children were among the rebel army – they stayed with their menfolk as protection from the marauding yeomen.

One of the leaders of the Wicklowmen in '98 was an extraordinary priest called Father Kearns who, on a visit to Paris during the French Revolution, had been taken prisoner and hanged from a lamppost but was of such huge stature that the lamppost had bent under his weight until his feet touched the ground. He subsequently escaped back to Ireland to take part in the rising there.

A devastating hail of musket and cannon fire from the government troops wreaked dreadful havoc among the attackers who soon began to falter. First the attack came to a halt and then the whole mass began to pull back, leaving hundreds of dead and wounded on the ground behind them. Nevertheless, the attackers regrouped and made two or three further charges but these also ended in failure.

Meanwhile on the coast the rebels were in a fierce fight with Needham's infantry and cavalry and had managed to get close to the defenders' barricade in front of the bridge. A number of desperate attacks on the barricade were unsuccessful, however, and the rebels were forced to draw back.

At the beginning Needham was so unnerved by the numbers of the rebels attacking and their perseverance in the face of devastating fire that he was on the point of retreating across the Avoca River. He changed his mind, however, when he got word that his defence on the Rock Road was holding out, and also noticed how effective was the withering fire from his men against the attackers on the Coolgreany Road.

Once more the rebels charged the Durham and Dumbarton men across the open ground before them but the result was still the same – the defenders' muskets and cannon killed large numbers before they could get close enough to use their fearsome pikes.

Father Michael Murphy was one of the casualties in one of these assaults and Esmond Kyan, the artillery man, was hit by a cannonball that carried away the remaining stump of his damaged arm.

Nothing seemed to be going in the insurgents' favour – they were making no progress on either the Coolgreany Road or the Rock Road. After four hours of effort they were

A man named Davies had an extraordinary escape from death on Vinegar Hill. When the rebels were searching for Protestants he had hidden in a privy for four days. His only source of food was a cock that had strayed into the privy and which he had eaten raw. He later left his hiding place but was captured and brought to the hill. There he was shot through his body, piked in the head and thrown into a shallow grave. Twelve hours later his own dog found him, scraped away his covering of earth and revived him by licking his face. His erstwhile 'executioners' took pity on him and brought him to a safe house.

The camp at Vinegar Hill was described thus:

> A scene of confusion and uproar . . . Great numbers of women were in the camp. Some men were employed in killing cattle, and boiling them in pieces in large copper brewing-pans; others were drinking, cursing and swearing; many of them were playing on musical instruments, which they had acquired by plunder in the adjacent Protestant houses.

becoming disheartened and by late evening the leaders decided to withdraw their men and abandon the attempt to take Arklow. The withdrawal proceeded fairly uneventfully on the left but the retreating troops at Rock Road were charged by the garrison's cavalry and suffered severe casualties.

The loss on the rebel side amounted to about 500 dead and many more hundreds wounded, while the garrison only lost about fifty men. The retreating rebels slowly made their way to Gorey, leaving behind them large numbers of their wounded comrades in the fields and ditches at the battle site.

The rebels had earlier established a huge camp on Vinegar Hill overlooking the town of Enniscorthy and after the defeat at Arklow it became their chief position. The weather at the time was so fine and dry that the lack of tents at night was no great hardship.

There was an old windmill on top of the hill on which the rebels had displayed the flag of rebellion. Thirty-five Protestant prisoners from Enniscorthy, accused of nothing more serious than having Orange sympathies, were housed in the windmill. Fifteen of them were now taken out and executed in a cruel and haphazard way by rebels armed with pikes and muskets; some were shot while others were attacked with the pikes. The wife of one of the prisoners found her husband still alive the next morning while a rebel with a scythe was moving through the bodies finishing off any who showed signs of life.

The Rebel Camp Comes Under Attack

General Lake (who had been appointed Commander-in-Chief of the army in March 1798 and moved to the Dublin area) now set about attacking the rebel camp. He had an army of 20,000 men in three divisions, one led by himself, another four miles away to the southwest, led by Lieutenant General Johnson, and a third, eight miles to the east, led by Needham.

Lake was anxious that the three divisions should attack at the same time and sent word to Needham to approach the hill with all speed on the east. He also sent word to Johnson to attack from the west, while he himself would attack from the north.

As soon as Needham got the word he started out immediately, under cover of darkness, and arrived near the hill by 2 a.m. His men were weary after their thirteen-kilometre march but Lake immediately ordered them to march around the hill to be in a position to cut off any retreat by the rebels in a southerly direction. Lake then brought his own troops to the northern side of Vinegar Hill. By this time he had about 10,000 troops under his immediate command and even though the rebels had greater numbers they were completely exhausted and had almost no ammunition.

When Lake's troops got into position on the northern slopes of the hill they started an artillery barrage against the rebel camp. The rebels had no effective means of reply except for a few unsuccessful cannon shots and were forced to withdraw as best they could out of range. They suffered many casualties from the explosive shells of the troopers and the men in the trenches along the face of the hill suffered several direct hits.

When daybreak came at about five o'clock, Lake halted the artillery bombardment and his infantry began a general assault. The rebels were in a desperate situation – they had little or no ammunition and the thousands of refugees in the camp, in their desire to be near their relatives, were in among the fighting men.

At seven o'clock Lake started an all-out assault on the hill from several directions at once. The Wexford pikemen did not passively defend their positions, however, but launched a spirited charge against their attackers. It came to nothing, though, for the soldiers counter-attacked and drove the rebels back up the hill.

When Perry and the other leaders saw that the position was hopeless he ordered the retreat at about nine o'clock. In order to prevent a total rout, they endeavoured to delay the advance of the enemy on the northern and eastern slopes. This they did with great courage so that their main body was able to move southwards in relative safety. When their comrades had got some distance down the hill the rearguards began to fall back themselves.

Many hundreds of refugees were not able to withdraw as quickly as the rebel army and Lake's cavalry charged in among the unarmed non-combatants, massacring any men in their path. Many women and children were also slaughtered, while more perished in the mad stampede to safety. Meanwhile the rebel army had had a stroke of luck because Needham's troops had not got into position to close off the route to the south. They were either too fatigued after their long march or else the route they took was too circuitous. Whatever the reason, the rebels were able to get away before Needham arrived, and when his troops were seen approaching from the east, some newly arrived rebel reinforcements immediately started to attack them. Eventually Needham gave up the pursuit of the retreating arm and they got clean away.

With the defeat at Vinegar Hill the insurrection could be said to be over. Some isolated bodies of insurgents still held out and resistance continued in some areas. Most of the remaining leaders were arrested and almost all of them ended up on the scaffold.

Most of the rebel army had no uniform but a shoe-black named Monk is described as wearing a horseman's jacket of green with crossed bands of silver lace across the front, green pantaloons trimmed with silver and a green cap with an ostrich feather – all taken from a plundered house.

The rebels carried pocketfuls of wheat to provide sustenance. A strange consequence of this was the amount of sprouting wheat to be seen on many of the shallow graves holding fallen rebels.

The escape route of the rebels from Vinegar Hill has since become known as Needham's Gap. The general himself was often referred to afterwards as 'General Needless' or the 'Late General Needham'.

INDEX